READY OR NOT

Preparing Today for a Young Woman's Tomorrow

SARA CARLSON

D1378035

Bill Rice Ranch Publications
Murfreesboro, TN 37128-4555

ABOUT THE AUTHOR AND THIS MINISTRY

Sara Carlson first came to the Bill Rice Ranch as a summer staff counselor from 1993-1995. She then spent one year teaching at Bill Rice Christian Academy. Her husband Troy, an evangelist, serves as the Director of West Branch of the Bill Rice Ranch, Williams, Arizona. The Carlsons, along with their two children, Abby and Nathan, spend their lives in revival work, both in camp programs and in week-long church meetings.

The Ranch was started over fifty years ago by Evangelist Bill and Cathy Rice as a way to reach the Deaf with the message of salvation. The Ranch now holds week-long camps all summer in three separate programs — Deaf, Junior, and Teen. These programs run simultaneously, allowing churches to bring young people from all three groups while only making one trip.

The truths of this book are heartfelt convictions, regularly preached from the pulpit of the Bill Rice Ranch. Whether dealing with teenagers, juniors, families or the Deaf, the Ranch's goal is to challenge people with revival truth.

For more information about the Bill Rice Ranch, please call 615-893-2767 or write to the Bill Rice Ranch, 627 Bill Rice Ranch Rd., Murfreesboro, TN 37128, or visit the website at www.billriceranch.org.

CONTENTS

FOREWORD

One fundamental key to the Christian life is applying the Word of God. If you cannot *apply* God's Word, then you are not going to *live by* it. If you do not *live by* it, then the Bible *is not* your authority in life. As a preacher, my goal is to communicate the Bible in such a way that it is clear and powerful, demanding a decision from the hearer. In the front flyleaf of one of my Bibles I have written, "Explain it. Illustrate it. Apply it."

That is exactly what you are about to read in this book. You will find truth after truth explained, illustrated, and applied. I dare say you will repeatedly be brought to the point of decision — good decisions which will help put you on or keep you on the path to success in your life.

Written in the front of another Bible from which I preach are these verses:

> *And my speech and my preaching was not with enticing words of man's wisdom, but in demonstration of the Spirit and of power: That your faith should not stand in the wisdom of men, but in the power of God.* I Corinthians 2:4-5

As you read this book, you don't have to take a human author's word for it. You can accept God's very words.

I have now read this book several times as my wife has prepared it. I have found it to be powerfully convicting and thoroughly helpful even though I am not a part of the target audience. Prayerfully, this book, received with an open heart, will be used as a tool of God to mold young women into God-honoring success stories. And may you be one of them!

Evangelist Troy Carlson

MAKING THE MOST OF THIS BOOK

With the completion of this book, my heart is burdened. For while all the effort put into writing it has come to an end, the true work has just begun: the work in you and me as readers. In whatever stage of life we find ourselves, we all need to be prepared to do God's bidding in our lives—and that will not be accomplished by accident. It is my prayer that the biblical truths presented in the following pages will stir you to take steps toward a successful, fulfilling life—both now and in the future.

Preparing for the future will not happen in one day. Neither will reading this book. So take your time; absorb all you can. Use the Journal Thoughts at the end of each chapter to make notes concerning how the Lord spoke to your heart. And in the days to come, go back to those notes to remind yourself of the truths you have learned and of the decisions you have made.

CHAPTER ONE

Here It Comes

Do you remember summer days when you were seven or eight—how long those days seemed? I would play outside from morning until dark, enjoying every moment of it. There was hide and seek, hopscotch, swimming, forts and tree houses, roller skating, jump rope, playgrounds, popsicles, and secret missions in the woods. Life was good; days seemed to last forever. But they didn't—for me or for you. What seems like just yesterday is now several years past. Some days may seem long and some short, but time passes at the same speed for all, regardless of age, stage of life, circumstances or anything else. And it passes quickly.

For what is your life? It is even a vapour, that appeareth for a little time, and then vanisheth away. James 4:14b

I have heard many older folks talk about how fast time passes. "It will be gone before you know it," they warn. "Enjoy every minute of it now."

As a youth, I did not give much thought to it all. "They are old, and I am young" was more or less my carefree attitude. But now I am beginning to understand what they were telling me; I am beginning to see that life is short. One does not need to be older, however, to accept this truth. The Bible states it clearly.

The days of our years are threescore years and ten; and if by reason of strength they be fourscore years, yet is their strength labour and sorrow; for it is soon cut off, and we fly away. Psalm 90:10

We live seventy years—if we are healthy, maybe eighty years—yet this life ends. It is over. It flies away. My grandfather lived a very long life of ninety-six years. Yet he died, and his life was but a vapor. The life that lives the very longest is still short. The longest summer day will still have an end. The Bible does not point out the brevity of life to cause us depression, but to emphasize that we need to make the most of the days we have.

So teach us to number our days, that we may apply our hearts unto wisdom. Psalm 90:12

Right now, tomorrow may seem like it will never arrive; but it will come and go. Ready or not—here it comes. Here comes tomorrow. Here comes your future. The question is: What are you doing to prepare for it?

What Your Future Does Not Need

Fretting

You are in a stage of life where it is very natural to think about the days to come. Many of my friends dreamed about their weddings as they discussed flowers, colors, dresses, and all the other details that go along with it. I was different. I did not think about my wedding much until it was time to plan it. But I did dream about my children and what I would name them. I wrote a list of names, narrowed it down, and picked out my favorites. Those types of dreams can be fun. We have hope for the future; we wonder about it. What will I do? Where will I live? Who will I marry? How many kids will I have? There are endless dreaming possibilities. You do, however, need to make sure your dreaming does not include fretting. The Bible is clear that we should not worry about tomorrow.

> *Therefore take no thought, saying, What shall we eat? or, What shall we drink? or, Wherewithal shall we be clothed?... Take therefore no thought for the morrow: for the morrow shall take thought for the things of itself. Sufficient unto the day is the evil thereof.* Matthew 6:31, 34

The word *thought* implies anxious thought. What if we do not have anything to eat, drink, or wear tomorrow! What will we do? Oh, no! Worry, worry, worry. Perhaps it seems unrealistic to you at this stage of life that one would worry about having food, drink, and raiment; but what about *these* worries? What if I do not find anyone to marry! What if I can't have children! What if God sends me to Africa! What if I can't get a job! Oh, no! Worry, worry, worry. There is no difference. While the focus of worry may change, worry is always the same. And it is always wrong. Do not let anxious thoughts have any part in your dreams for the future.

Be careful for nothing; but in every thing by prayer and supplication with thanksgiving let your requests be made known unto God. Philippians 4:6

In the first part of the verse, God tells us not to be anxious about anything. To worry is to sin. Do not accept anxiety as no big deal. If, when you dream about the future, your thoughts include worry, then your thinking about the future is not Bible thinking. Deal with worry as sin and do not welcome it into your thoughts and life.

The second half of the verse tells what we are to do instead of worrying. Pray. I have heard it said many times that if you can worry about it, then you can pray about it. That is true. Prayer is exactly what God wants us to do with our concerns. When I find myself fretting, I need to first confess the sin to God, ask Him to give me victory, and then bring my concern to him in prayer. Worry has no power to control circumstances or futures, but the God of prayer does.

Boasting

Boast not thyself of to morrow; for thou knowest not what a day may bring forth. Proverbs 27:1

Go to now, ye that say, To day or to morrow we will go into

*such a city, and continue there a year, and buy and sell, and
get gain: Whereas ye know not what shall be on the morrow.
For what is your life? It is even a vapour, that appeareth for a
little time, and then vanisheth away. For that ye ought to say,
If the Lord will, we shall live, and do this, or that.*
James 4:13-15

How foolish these people were to make plans about the
future without regard for God's will! They were proud of
the fact that they were going to do what *they* wanted to do.
They did not recognize that their life was not their own —
that their future was not in their control.

I was alone in an airport waiting to board my plane. There
was not much to do but watch people. (That is really the
most interesting thing to do in an airport anyway!) Two
teen girls walked into my gate area and sat down nearby —
close enough for me to hear the conversation they struck
up with an older lady. These girls were pretty, stylishly
dressed, bright, and incredibly outgoing. They mentioned
that they were headed to California. They were on spring
break and had an agenda. It was their chance to get on the
big screen. They were going to Hollywood expecting to be
noticed by the movie crowd. These unsaved, I assume, teen
girls boasted about their future, giving no regard to God.
We would not really expect anything different from those
who have never placed their faith in Christ for salvation.
Yet many Christian young people are guilty of the same
boasting concerning their own dreams and thoughts of
the future. "Once I get done with high school, I am going
to college for two years to get a secretarial degree. I will
get a job, meet the man of my dreams, and get married. I

will only work two years because then I will have my first baby...." The plans go on and on. Have you, like the people in James, set an agenda; or are you acknowledging God's hand in your future? Are you seeking what *you* want in life, or are you determined to follow God's plan?

> *The ground of a certain rich man brought forth plentifully: And he thought within himself, saying, What shall I do, because I have no room where to bestow my fruits? And he said, This will I do: I will pull down my barns, and build greater; and there will I bestow all my fruits and my goods. And I will say to my soul, Soul, thou hast much goods laid up for many years; take thine ease, eat, drink, and be merry. But God said unto him, Thou fool, this night thy soul shall be required of thee: then whose shall those things be, which thou hast provided? So is he that layeth up treasure for himself, and is not rich toward God.* Luke 12:16b-21

There are many truths in this passage, and one is definitely that we should not boast of the future. Our dreams ought to be surrounded by surrender to God's will.

What Your Future Needs

My son and I were playing a quick game of hide-and-seek. It was his turn to count—to thirty. Now let me stop and say that I am a nice counter—dragging out every number so that my children will have plenty of time to hide. But not my son. He counts like an auctioneer! To make matters worse, I had not thought of a good hiding place ahead of time. I was standing in the middle of the living room when I heard, "Ready or not, here I come!" I dashed behind a chair with my feet obviously poking out behind. He stepped out of the bedroom and exclaimed, "Found you!" Game over. I was not ready, and I lost.

The bell rings. You get yourself comfortable in your desk, set for a long lecture about the Civil War. You reach for your textbook when you notice that no one else is reaching for his book, but everyone is getting out a pen and paper. Suddenly. a sickening feeling comes into your stomach. That feeling worsens as you remember that today is history test day. You forgot. You did not study. You were not prepared.

All of us can probably relate to a similar experience. We know that pit-in-the-stomach feeling that comes with not being ready for something important. We can be distraught by not being ready for an exam yet often give little thought to being prepared for what God has for us in days to come. We do not know what the future holds; our lives are in God's hands. That truth should not, however, promote a careless attitude that says, "Well, God will do whatever He wants with me, so there is no need to do anything today to be ready for tomorrow." The acknowledgement of God's omnipotence (complete power) in our lives should drive us to prepare ourselves to be ready to do His will tomorrow.

> *Go to the ant, thou sluggard; consider her ways, and be wise: Which having no guide, overseer, or ruler, Provideth her meat in the summer, and gathereth her food in the harvest. How long wilt thou sleep, O sluggard? when wilt thou arise out of thy sleep?* Proverbs 6:6-9

We are to learn from the ants. They gather while there is time and food, so they will have what is needed in days to come. As a young woman, you should not be lazy but take advantage of this time you have and the means you have to learn, grow, and be prepared for your future.

The many God-fearing, courageous men and women of the Bible were not born ready for the tasks God had planned for them. If they had not followed God's leading and commands in tasks that seemed insignificant at the time, they would not have been ready to do huge things for God later in their lives. Samuel spent his childhood serving Eli in the temple. It was a time of preparation for him—a time of learning God's Word and applying it. Noah would not have been ready for the Flood had he not prepared by building the ark. Elisha learned from Elijah; he needed that time of preparation. After Paul's sight was restored, he spent *"certain days with the disciples which were at Damascus"* (Acts 9:19). No doubt these days played a great role in Paul's being ready to fulfill God's plan. The disciples of Jesus spent years at his feet learning and preparing for ministry.

While young women certainly can serve God now, this stage of your life is mostly a time of preparation. Not being ready for a test may result in a failing grade. Not being hidden by the time the counter yells out, "Ready or not, here I come!" will result in losing the game. Not being prepared for life will result in disappointment, despair, and devastation. The stakes are high. Ready or not, the future is coming!

JOURNAL THOUGHTS

❑   I have been worrying about the future. I realize that I need to confess that as sin and begin praying about these concerns:

❑   I have been planning out my future without regard to God's will. I need to surrender these desires of mine to Him:

❑   I have not been making the best use of this time of preparation in my life. I need to be more diligent in these specific areas:

CHAPTER TWO

Know That You Know

My husband has preached a message mentioning that people have all sorts of fears: fear of heights, fear of snakes, fear of mice, fear of the dark. But he says that perhaps the worst fear is a fear of the unknown. Then he tells of a time when this fear of "not knowing" gripped our hearts as parents.

Our daughter Abby was only a couple months old when we noticed a small bump on her head. At first we were not concerned, assuming that we had clumsily caused the bump. We were new parents and not accustomed to handling a baby. We thought we must have bumped her head on the carrying bar of her car seat. But the bump did not go away; in fact, it seemed to be getting bigger. We took Abby to her pediatrician and were referred to a specialist who took an x-ray. There was a definite growth, and surgery was scheduled. Four days prior to surgery, Abby had a CT scan to determine if the growth was connected to her brain. If so, her surgery would be brain surgery; if not, then it would be a simple cosmetic procedure.

We had to wait for the results of the CT scan until the day of surgery. Those four days were filled with the terrible fear of not knowing. Would our baby be facing major brain surgery? The uncertainty was tormenting.

Many people face an even greater doubt and torment every time they think about their future in eternity. "Will I go to heaven? Am I really saved?" They are not completely certain, not 100% sure, of their eternal life. They have questions that plague their minds. No one should have to face this uncertainty with a nagging doubt in the back of her mind. No area of preparing for the future is more important than being sure you are on your way to heaven. The good news is that God does not want anyone to struggle with doubts. His Word shows us how we can be confident and rid ourselves of these doubts forever. The feeling of relief we felt when we were told that our baby would be fine scarcely compares to the relief you can have concerning your eternity.

I was talking with a lady and asked her if she knew where she would go when she died. She answered, "I think to heaven—I hope." I then asked her why she thought she would go to heaven. She replied that she had lived a good life, had gone to church, and thought she would be allowed into heaven based on how she lived. But her reasoning was not based on the Bible. In fact, the Bible tells us that our good works—the things we do to try to gain favor with God—are repulsive to Him.

But we are all as an unclean thing, and all our righteousnesses are as filthy rags; and we all do fade as a leaf; and our iniquities, like the wind, have taken us away. Isaiah 64:6

We are in sad shape, according to this verse, since any good thing that we try to do is viewed by God as disgusting rags. This woman's church-going and good life are not acceptable to God. He sees her works as an unclean thing.

For all have sinned, and come short of the glory of God. Romans 3:23

For I say unto you, That except your righteousness shall exceed the righteousness of the scribes and Pharisees, ye shall in no case enter into the kingdom of heaven. Matthew 5:20

The Bible says that all of us fall short of God's requirements for heaven. The scribes and Pharisees lived very clean lives. They lived by the law. They spent their days trying to do good. Yet Jesus said that no one will enter heaven unless they live more righteously than these upright people did. He was not saying you must try harder to live better. He was showing us how impossible it is. There is no hope in good works if they must exceed those of the scribes and Pharisees! Eternal life in heaven is impossible to attain by works!

Now to him that worketh is the reward not reckoned of grace, but of debt. But to him that worketh not, but believeth on him that justifieth the ungodly, his faith is counted for righteousness. Romans 4:4-5

For by grace are ye saved through faith; and that not of yourselves: it is the gift of God: Not of works, lest any man should boast. Ephesians 2:8-9

These verses and many more say that heaven cannot be reached by *doing* anything. Going to church to gain favor with God is a work. Trying to be a kind person to gain favor with God is a work. Giving money in an offering plate to gain favor with God is a work. Being baptized or confirmed to gain favor with God is a work. Anything that we do—anything that we depend upon besides His free gift to us—to gain favor with God so we may enter heaven is not acceptable with God. So the question is: What is acceptable?

To the praise of the glory of his grace, wherein he hath made us accepted in the beloved. In whom we have redemption through his blood, the forgiveness of sins, according to the riches of his grace. Ephesians 1:6-7

Jesus Christ is acceptable. His atonement, or full payment for our sin, is acceptable. When Jesus, Who is God Himself, gave His life on the cross, He made His righteousness available to us.

For he [God] *hath made him* [Jesus] *to be sin for us, who knew no sin; that we might be made the righteousness of God in him.* II Corinthians 5:21

We can have the righteousness of Christ. That righteousness is acceptable to God and makes eternal life in heaven not only possible but guaranteed! The way a person gains the righteousness of Christ is simply by receiving it as a free gift. Jesus did the work—He died on the cross and rose from the dead. Ephesians says that eternal life is the gift of God. It is by grace—God's doing for us what we could not possibly do for ourselves. It is obtained through faith. When you receive a gift you simply reach out your hands and take it. It is then yours. You cannot reach out your hands and physically take and hold the gift of Christ. But receiving righteousness and eternal life is that simple. Accept the gift by faith. John 3:16 is one of the most well-known verses in the Bible, yet many people do not understand what it is saying. *Whosoever believeth in him should not perish, but have everlasting life.* Anyone who makes the decision to believe in what Christ did as payment for her sins (something that we cannot do ourselves) and puts her dependence in Him alone has eternal life. This decision to trust Christ can be verbalized by a prayer like this:

> *God, I know that I am a sinner as the Bible teaches and that all the things I try to do to gain favor with you are not acceptable. I realize that only being perfect is acceptable to you and that Jesus' blood made a way for me to be perfect in your sight. I believe that and am depending on what He did on the cross to remove my sins and make me acceptable for heaven. Amen*

A person that has made this decision is what the Bible calls "saved"—saved from sin and the penalty of it.

Perhaps you are a person who has never made this decision. You know that you have been trusting in something else besides Jesus Christ and Him alone for your salvation and eternity. You can make the decision to trust Christ right now. I hope that you will.

Still Uncertain?

Maybe you have made the decision to depend on Christ for salvation in the past but still struggle with doubts about it. You feel tormented, wondering if you are really saved. Maybe you are not sure you "really meant it." Or perhaps you cannot remember much detail about it. It could be that you just do not feel saved or have struggles with sin that cause doubts. Whatever the cause of uncertainty, there is hope to end the battle. You can know that you are saved. You are not alone in this battle. Many, including the people in I John, have fought with these doubts. Listen to why John wrote to these people in this short but powerful book.

> *These things have I written unto you that believe on the name of the Son of God; that ye may know that ye have eternal life, and that ye may believe on the name of the Son of God.*
> I John 5:13

There is no doubt that John would want to convince anyone who had never trusted Christ as Savior to make that decision. But he writes to believers here, to people who have already made the decision to depend on Christ for eternal life. He says that he is writing to believers that they may know that they are saved—to end all doubting. John points those who struggle with doubting back to the truth of the Word of God concerning salvation. He writes:

> *And this is the record, that God hath given to us eternal life,*
> *and this life is in his Son. He that hath the Son hath life; and*
> *he that hath not the Son of God hath not life.* I John 5:11-12

The question that needs to be asked is not "How do you feel?" or "How good is your life?" or anything other than "Do you have the Son?" Obviously, we cannot physically grab Jesus and have Him. So, what does that mean? In the Gospel of John the Bible tells us how we have the Son.

> *But as many as received him, to them gave he power to become*
> *the sons of God, even to them that believe on his name.*
> John 1:12

We have the Son by receiving Him, believing in Him, depending on Him for removal of sins, and trusting in Him for eternal life. These are different words which mean the same thing. It is placing your faith in Christ to do for you what you cannot do for yourself. When you struggle with doubts about your salvation, you need to set everything else aside and ask yourself the question, "Have I placed my faith in Christ and Him alone for eternal life?" **If the answer is no**, then you are not saved and not on your way to heaven. But you can be saved if you will make that decision. **If you are not sure**, perhaps you just cannot remember if there was a time in your life when you placed your faith in Christ for salvation, then you can make sure today. You could express your thoughts in a prayer like this:

God, I cannot remember if I have trusted in Jesus to remove my sins and give me a home in heaven. I am just not sure. I do not want to have any doubt, and so I am making that decision today. I am deciding to depend on what Jesus did on the cross to make me acceptable for heaven.

There is no need to make that decision over and over again; it is a one time decision with eternal ramifications. You can know you have eternal life without doubt.

If the answer is yes, then you have the Son and thereby have eternal life. You are saved. It is not uncommon, however, for believers to say, "Yes, I have trusted Christ as my Savior, but…." But what? It could be a number of things.

"But I can't remember exactly what I said when I trusted Christ as Savior."

I do not remember the words I spoke when I was saved as a young girl. The promise of the Bible is not that you have eternal life if you remember the words you spoke as you trusted Christ as Savior. A person can be saved without ever uttering a word. The promise is that if you have the Son, then you have eternal life. Yes, you do need to know that you have placed your dependence in Christ, but you do not need to know the words you spoke.

"But I am not sure I said the right thing."

You are in good company. The thief on the cross who trusted Jesus for eternal life right before he died, spoke very unimpressive words to express the decision of his heart.

And he said unto Jesus, Lord, remember me when thou comest into thy kingdom. And Jesus said unto him, Verily I say unto thee, to day shalt thou be with me in paradise.
Luke 23:42-43

Jesus knew the heart of the thief, and He knows yours as well. My daughter was saved when she was very young. She prayed with childlike faith something like this: "Dear Jesus, I know I sin and do bad things. Please save me and take me to heaven. Amen." Though her prayer was not theologically deep, she certainly understood that she could not get to heaven on her own and knew that only Jesus could do that for her. Salvation does not come by saying "the right thing." It comes when one places her dependence on Christ to make her acceptable in the sight of God.

"But I am not sure I meant it."
If you prayed a prayer just to get someone off your back but did not place your dependence on Christ for eternity, then you are not saved. You need to trust Christ. But if you did place your faith in Christ knowing you could not save yourself, you are saved.

Evangelist Bill Rice III has used an illustration of a drowning man, a man that cannot swim, who is in huge trouble and knows it. He goes under the water and struggles to get back up. When he does he manages to yell, **"HELP!"** The lifeguard does not stand at the edge of the pool and ask, "Did you really mean your call for help?" Absurd, isn't it! The lifeguard who is in the business of saving people is not going to question a drowning man's call for help. As Bill

Rice III would say, "It is all over but the shouting." When a person confronts the sin problem, realizing she is in trouble and cannot save herself, and calls out for help placing her trust in Christ, she is saved. Do not play mind games with your salvation. If you have trusted Christ to save you from sin, then you have eternal life.

"But I just don't feel saved."

Being emotional creatures, we ladies can especially struggle with this. Emotions are good; God created them. I have a lot of them. Even my daughter at age five had an abundance of them. One day I found her crying in her room. I went to console her and asked what was wrong. Her answer: "I…(sob)…don't… (sob)…know." Although God intended for us to have emotions—and they play a big part in our personality—they have no part in determining salvation! We may have shown emotion at salvation or prior to it. We may have cried, laughed, felt joy, or expressed a number of other feelings. But the salvation decision is a matter of the will. It is a decision. Maybe you do not feel saved. I have felt that way before. But my salvation is not based on how I feel, and yours is not either. Claim I John 5:13. If you have placed your faith in Christ for salvation, then remind yourself that you do have the Son.

"But I still struggle with sin."

So did Paul. In Romans 7 he said that in his flesh was no good thing. The good things that he wanted to do, he did not do; and the bad that he did not want to do, he did. When we trust Christ, we are saved from the penalty of sin. But the presence of sin still remains. Paul speaks of two natures within a believer. The first is the carnal or the flesh which desires to fulfill all the lusts of the body without restraint. The second is spiritual or the part that can do no sin. A believer's life is a battle between the two.

> *For the flesh lusteth against the Spirit, and the Spirit against the flesh: and these are contrary the one to the other: so that ye cannot do the things that ye would.* Galatians 5:17

We have victory over sin when we submit to the Spirit Who cannot sin. We fall into sin when we submit to the old carnal man. It is God's desire that we have victory over sin, but the victory is not the basis of our salvation. Salvation is not based on how we live. A struggle with sin does not mean you are not saved. Sin was the reason we needed salvation by grace through faith. When God looks at a person who has trusted in Christ as Savior, He no longer sees sin but the righteousness of Christ.

> *For he hath made him to be sin for us, who knew no sin; that we might be made the righteousness of God in him.*
> II Corinthians 5:21

If I were to ask you if you have trusted Christ as Savior, would your answer be **"Yes, but..."**? Put aside the "but" and claim assurance based on God's Word.

Grow that You May Know

The Bible gives several ways in which you as a believer can

help yourself in the matter of assurance of salvation. The most important one is to claim the assurance based on the Word of God. We need to have that knowledge. We need to memorize verses about it. We need to read Scripture about salvation often. If you have trusted Christ as Savior but struggle with assurance of salvation, you need to spend much time with the verses quoted in the previous paragraphs. Read them over and over. Memorize them so that when the attack of doubt comes, you will be prepared with the Word of God. There are other things that can help with victory over doubts as well.

> *And beside this, giving all diligence, add to your faith virtue; and to virtue knowledge; And to knowledge temperance; and to temperance patience; and to patience godliness; And to godliness brotherly kindness; and to brotherly kindness charity. For if these things be in you, and abound, they make you that ye shall neither be barren nor unfruitful in the knowledge of our Lord Jesus Christ. But he that lacketh these things is blind, and cannot see afar off, and hath forgotten that he was purged from his old sins. Wherefore the rather, brethren, give diligence to make your calling and election sure: for if ye do these things, ye shall never fall.*
> II Peter 1:5-10

Here Peter tells believers that they need to add things to their faith so that they will not be unfruitful in the knowledge of Christ. He is not saying we need to add these things to our faith to become saved or more saved. We are to add these things so that we will have full assurance of our salvation. Growing as believers will give us a confidence of our salvation; it will help chase doubting away. We need to add to our faith, or grow, in these ways:

Virtue:	moral excellence; fulfilling God's purpose
Knowledge:	learning God's Word
Temperance:	self-control
Patience:	endurance; consistency
Godliness:	God-likeness; living a holy life that matches up with the Bible
Brotherly Kindness:	selflessly acting and speaking kindly; serving others
Charity:	love; doing what is right with a proper heart attitude

Unfortunately, after some people are saved, they do not add these things to their lives — they do not grow. They do not live a pure life that is separated from the world. They do not seek after knowledge by learning the Bible. Since they have not forced their flesh into submission, their flesh has complete control of what takes place. There is no endurance or consistency in their lives. They are far from being holy. They live selfishly without regard of others. They have not made the decision to love other people by doing right by them. **They doubt their salvation.** According to II Peter 1:9, they can even forget that they were saved.

There is a young lady who has come to camp for several years. Each summer she comes to talk with a counselor about her salvation. By her own testimony, she has placed her dependence on Christ for salvation but struggles with doubts about it. She is not sure that she is really saved. Why does she doubt if she has made the decision to trust Christ as her Savior? I believe the primary reason for her doubt is her lack of growth. She has worldly friends who encourage her to live sinfully. Instead of hating sin, she embraces it: she has not added virtue to her faith. During the year, she is not faithfully attending church. She is not reading the Word of God or hearing it preached on a consistent basis: she is not adding knowledge. She has not learned to control her lusts, but submits to every desire her flesh has: she has not added temperance. There is nothing upon which to build patience. Her life is not characterized by godliness. She is selfish instead of kind. It appears she loves no one but herself. Because she has not added to her faith, she doubts she ever had faith in the first place. Her problem, however, is not that she is not saved, but that she is not living like she is saved.

When you live a life of disobedience to God, you are pushing your assurance out the door. You will not have confidence of your salvation if you refuse to do right. Again, living in obedience is not the test of your salvation—the Word of God is. If you have trusted in Jesus to do for you what you cannot do for yourself concerning sin and eternity, then, according to the book of I John, you have eternal life. But adding and growing is essential to victory over doubts about salvation and victory in living the Christian life.

JOURNAL THOUGHTS

❑   I realize I have never placed my trust in Christ to make me acceptable for heaven, and I am making that decision today.

DATE:_____

−OR−

❑   I have already placed my trust in Christ for eternity and have confident assurance about my salvation.

−OR−

❑   I have already placed my trust in Christ for eternity but have struggled with doubts because...

❑   Today I am claiming assurance of my salvation based on the Bible and God's promises. I have already trusted Christ as my Savior, and I know that I am saved. I realize my salvation is not based on my life, feelings, or anything else but is based upon Christ and my dependence on Him.

DATE:_____

❑   I can see from II Peter 1 that there are things I need to add to my faith. I need to grow as a Christian in these areas:

CHAPTER THREE

The Rules of the Game

My family and I enjoy playing games. One of our favorites is Outburst®. Whenever we get together with people who have never played Outburst® before, my husband loves to read the following from the rules sheet to them:

> *This game is unfair! It is possible for there to be more than 10 appropriate answers for a topic. You may think of one that is not on the list. Toooooooooo bad! To paraphrase one former government official, "YOU NO MAKKA THE GAME, YOU NO MAKKA THE RULES!"*

You need to acknowledge in your life that since you no makka the game, you no makka the rules. You did not create the world. You did not create yourself. You had no part in making life. You also have no part in making the rules for it. God did. And He has provided all we need to know in His rule book — the Bible.

All scripture is given by inspiration of God, and is profitable for doctrine, for reproof, for correction, for instruction in righteousness: That the man of God may be perfect, throughly furnished unto all good works. II Timothy 3:16-17

The Bible is the living Word of God. It is His will for us. It is perfect and complete. The Bible is unlike any other book. All other books, including this one, are written by people who have sinned. They contain error. The Bible, however, is perfect. While books written using the Word of God may be helpful to us, none is as helpful as the Bible itself.

For the word of God is quick, and powerful, and sharper than any twoedged sword, piercing even to the dividing asunder of soul and spirit, and of the joints and marrow, and is a discerner of the thoughts and intents of the heart.
Hebrews 4:12

The Bible is profitable — for you. It will help you in your life to know truth, to know what is right and wrong, to know conviction of sin, to know how to deal with sin and make things right, to know how to live a life pleasing to God. The Word of God tells you how to be ready to do all God's will. The Bible can lead you into a joyful, victorious, and successful life. Its profit for you, however, is limited. It is limited by you. If you do not use the Bible, you obviously will not be helped by it. I wear contact lenses. Without them I could not drive, at least not safely. Without them I could not see the clock across the room. Without them I could not recognize my own children in the neighbor's yard. Those contact lenses are so important to me. It would be crazy of me to leave them in their case on the counter day after day without using them. There they would be of no profit to me. They would do me no good. The Bible is profitable — much more than my contact lenses. It is written so that we can know God. It is written so that we can know what God wants for us. It is written to give us the rules for a wonderful life and to guide us in that life. It tells us everything that we need to know. But just as my contacts do me no good on the counter, so the Bible does you little good on your counter.

> *This book of the law shall not depart out of thy mouth; but thou shalt meditate therein day and night, that thou mayest observe to do according to all that is written therein: for then thou shalt make thy way prosperous, and then thou shalt have good success.* Joshua 1:8

Notice the word *then* in this verse. To have a prosperous way and good success is dependent upon your doing something with the Bible. We often are quick to say how important the Bible is but slow to make it a part of our lives. The Bible is supreme. It is more valuable than silver and gold. Can you see that it is essential for you? Make it supreme in your life.

Read It!

Often I find myself guilty of skipping over or quickly skimming Bible verses in supplemental books that I read. Maybe that has been true for you as well even in this book. Shame on us! We treat the words of some man as more important than the words of God. In order to say what the psalmist said, we must read it.

> *Thy word have I hid in mine heart, that I might not sin against thee....Thy word is a lamp unto my feet, and a light unto my path.* Psalm 119:11, 105

> *Moreover by them is thy servant warned: and in keeping of them there is great reward.* Psalm 19:11

You will not know right from wrong without it. You will not know God's leading in your life without it. You will not know wisdom without it. You will not know victory over sin without it. You will not know good success without it. You must read it.

Habits are often bad. They can be really bad. I remember a couple of kids in elementary school whose reputations suffered because of their bad habits. But not all habits are bad. In fact, you need to establish a good habit — the habit of making the Bible a part of your daily life.

Read the Bible every day.

You need to read some of God's Word every day. While it is true that some days you will have time to read only a few verses, most days you will have time for more. I think it would be wise of you to read one Psalm, one chapter of Proverbs, and one-half to one full chapter of John each day. It will take you several weeks to read all the way through those books, but read them beginning to end. When you finish the book of John, begin a different book. When you finish Proverbs or Psalms, start reading them over again.

Allow this pattern to become a habit in your life.

Read it at the same time each day.

I have found that if I have not scheduled reading the Bible into my day, then I do not do it. It helps tremendously to set a specific time aside for doing it. Be determined to do it at the same time each day for so long that it becomes natural. Most people eat meals at the same time each day. When the clock turns to lunch hour, we do not have to ask ourselves, "What should I do now?" We just automatically head to the table. Make it so that when the clock chimes that special time, you automatically head to your Bible. While morning is likely best, pick a time that will work for you. It may mean getting up a little earlier each day. Do it if that is what it will take.

Read it away from distractions.

Pick a quiet, private place that will not likely have interruptions. I know that can be challenging. If it becomes impossible, consider changing the time of your reading to make it possible. If you are sleepy, do not lie down while you read. Turn off music and television. Close the blinds if movement outside is taking your attention. If there is something that can be done about the distraction, do it. Make the atmosphere for reading your Bible the best that it can be.

Get back at it.

It can be discouraging to miss a day of Bible reading. It is even more discouraging to allow that to turn into several days. Several days will soon form a new habit—the habit of not reading the Bible at all. Have you missed a day? Get back at it. Have you missed several days? Get back at it. Have you missed so much that it is a lot of work to even think about it? Get back at it.

Take it in.

While it is a good habit to automatically head to your Bible each day, it is a bad one to automatically read it. There is no point in taking time each day to open God's Word if you are not going to pay attention to what you are reading. All of us have read entire pages of textbooks before realizing that while we were reading, we were somewhere else in dreamland. While that is an easy habit to form, it is a very bad one. When I catch myself at the end of a chapter not having any idea of what I just read, I know that it did not count. I start the chapter over again, careful not to waste any more time on daydreaming. Just as it is helpful to take notes in class to ensure you stay in the same hemisphere, it can be helpful to take notes while reading the Bible. Read out loud if that will be a help to you. Discipline yourself to take in what you are reading.

Hear It!

> *For the preaching of the cross is to them that perish foolishness; but unto us which are saved it is the power of God.* I Corinthians 1:18

Did you know the Bible is full of preaching? Many chapters contain sermons. The Bible records a message that the martyr Stephen preached. Several of Paul's messages are found in the book of Acts. The Lord Jesus preached to both huge crowds and small groups as found in the four Gospels. If God Himself used the preaching of His Word to communicate truth, it would make sense that it is important. Being under the sound preaching of the Word of God is an essential part of making the Bible supreme in your life.

Preaching will help you tremendously in several ways.
1. To know the Bible
Every time you sit under accurate biblical preaching, you will know the Bible a little better. A good preacher will take a verse, several verses, or a passage and read it, explain it, and make it clear. You may hear stories of the Old Testament come alive. You may hear of the adventures of Paul. You may hear of the miracles of Christ. You may hear time and time again the precious Gospel of Jesus Christ. And each time you do, you will know it better. Whatever the verse, whatever the topic — the preaching of God's Word will help you know it.

2. To understand the Bible
Hearing the preaching of God's Word will help you understand it. There have been hundreds of times when biblical preaching has opened my eyes to truth. Most of the truths I share in this book I have learned from Bible preaching. In Acts 8, there is an amazing story of an unsaved man who was sitting in his chariot reading the Bible.

Then the Spirit said unto Philip, Go near, and join thyself to this chariot. And Philip ran thither to him, and heard him read

the prophet Esaias, and said, Understandest thou what thou readest? And he said, How can I, except some man should guide me? And he desired Philip that he would come up and sit with him....Then Philip opened his mouth, and began at the same scripture, and preached unto him Jesus.
Acts 8:29-31, 35

After hearing the preaching of the Word of God, the man was saved. Unquestionably, a person can read the Bible for herself and be saved. Unquestionably, a believer can read the Bible for herself and understand it. And unquestionably, a person can hear the preaching of the Bible and have it help her understanding.

3. To be persuaded by the Bible

The purpose of preaching is to persuade listeners to biblical truth. When a preacher stands before you, it is his goal to convince you of a truth or truths from the Bible. He wants that Bible conviction to become your Bible conviction. If there is sin in your life, he wants to give conviction of the sin and persuade you to deal with it. If there is an area of growth that needs to be added to your life, the preacher wants you to be consumed with that need. I heard a message preached to young children about the need for the Bible in their lives. That preacher told the kids that the Bible is different than any other book. He convinced them that it is supremely special. He showed them that it is important that they begin reading the Bible every day. It was obvious that the preaching of God's Word helped those kids. For some who already read their Bibles every day it made the necessity of it concrete in their mind. Many saw for the first time the need for the Bible in their lives. Those kids heard Bible preaching and were persuaded by it. And the result was good. It is good for you as well. It is an essential part of your growth as a believer. The conviction does not feel good; I have never enjoyed coming face to face with sin while listening to the Bible being preached. It is not pleasant to be convinced of my wickedness. Often I do not like the truth about which I am being confronted because it conflicts with my fleshly desires. But I am so thankful for it all. Without the conviction (convincing) I have received from the preaching of God's Word, I would be living a miserable, unhappy and wicked life. It is so easy to mentally fight the persuasion of preaching. Our flesh never wants to be confronted. Do not push preaching away. Embrace it, knowing that the conviction it brings is a key to victory in your life.

Make preaching work for you.
1. Be there.
Sunday mornings of revival meetings, my husband often encourages the crowd to come every night of that week. He tells them that he has spent lots of money doing a study. And after much time spent on this study, it has revealed that those who come to the revival meetings are more likely to be helped by the preaching than those who do not come. (He has not really spent time and money on this study!) It is common sense, is it not? Obviously, you will not be helped by preaching if you do not hear it. So be there. Be where? Wherever there is good Bible preaching. Go to Sunday school and hear the Bible preached. Go to Sunday morning and evening services. Go to the midweek service. Go to youth group activities. Go to a Bible-preaching camp.

Go every night of revival meetings in your church. Go to missions conferences, special weekend conferences, and retreats. As often as possible, hear the Bible preached. The more you do, the more you will know, understand, and be persuaded by it.

2. Listen.

I have been in a number of services when nearby a group of teens whispered or passed notes all through the preaching. Those teens received no help from the Bible in those services. They were there, but they did not listen. There have been times when my mind was so consumed with other things that I did not concentrate on hearing preaching. I was there, but I did not listen. If you are in services but do not listen, you will not be helped. Again it is common sense. We could so often have help for our lives and our futures if we would only listen. Listen to the preaching of the Bible. If you fight being sleepy during services, go to bed earlier the night before. Take notes to help keep your mind from daydreaming. Sit away from friends who are a distraction to you. Train and discipline yourself to listen. Determine to learn something from every message you hear.

3. Make decisions.

As you listen to Bible preaching, make decisions. If you are confronted with sin, confess it. If you are challenged to witness to your unsaved friends, decide to do it. Apply the truths you hear to your life. Do not put off making decisions until later. The conviction may lessen by the time you get home, and the decision you intended to make will likely never be made. When you are confronted by truth but fail to take that truth and apply it personally to your life, you have missed out on the benefits of that truth. One of the saddest stories of missed benefits is in Acts 26. Paul, a prisoner, was defending himself before King Agrippa. In his defense, he preached Christ.

> *Then Agrippa said unto Paul, Almost thou persuadest me to be a Christian.* Acts 26:28

When confronted with his need to be saved, King Agrippa refused to be persuaded. When he rejected Christ, he missed the most important benefit: sins forgiven and a home in heaven. Yet in the same way many believers miss benefits like joy, answered prayer, victory, peace, and living in the will of God because they refuse to apply the truths they have heard. In their hearts, they answer the preaching of the Bible with, "I'm almost persuaded to be baptized. I'm almost persuaded to read the Bible. I'm almost persuaded to get rid of my sinful entertainment. I'm almost persuaded to confess my pride. I'm almost persuaded to witness to my neighbor." What you do with the preaching of God's Word will have a great affect on your life now and in the future.

4. Get help.
Some of the closest times together for my husband and me have been when we shared with each other the truths, the convictions, and the decisions we made after hearing preaching. While that closeness is special, the help it provides is even greater. I gain someone to pray with me about the matter. I gain someone to encourage me in that decision in the days to come. I gain some extra accountability. I can ask

questions when I have them. How it helps to have someone else know about the decision! Though you are not married, you can have that same help. Before you leave church, ask your pastor's wife to pray with you about your decision. You can ask her questions you may have. Talk to your parents and ask them to help you follow through with your decision. Share the decision with a friend who can encourage you later on.

After hearing several Bible messages, a young lady made a decision to go to Christian college the next year. She told several people including her pastor, her parents, and several friends of her decision. When preparations became complicated and expenses increased, it would have been a great temptation to question the decision to go. But there was a group of people who knew about the decision. They were there to pray about the needs. They were there to encourage her that God could take care of all the details. They reminded her of the importance of the decision. She went and had a great year. But I wonder what would have happened if, after making the decision to go, she did not share that decision with anyone. Would the complications have kept her from following through had she not had the support of others? I do not know, but the support and encouragement was certainly a help. You can have that same type of support and encouragement in your decisions if you ask for it. Why try to do battle alone when you can have help?

Know It!

Reading the Bible and hearing it preached will certainly get you on your way to knowing the Word of God. Once you are in the habit of reading every day and hearing preaching as often as possible, continue in that growth by making it an intrinsic part of your life.

> *Thy word have I hid in mine heart, that I might not sin against thee....I will meditate in thy precepts, and have respect unto thy ways. I will delight myself in thy statutes: I will not forget thy word.* Psalm 119:11, 15-16

Hide it.

Do you remember having treasures as a young girl? Maybe you found pretty rocks that seemed to be jewels. Whatever the trinket, it was special—so special that you did the only natural thing with it. You hid it. That treasure needed just the right home—a place where no one else would find it. You needed to protect it from little brothers, nosey neighbors, and clutter-hating mothers. The psalmist did the same thing—except it was no trinket he hid. He so valued the Word of God that he hid it in the safest place he knew—his heart. He could not lose or have stolen what was laid up there. It was there and ready whenever he needed it. And he needed it in his heart to keep that same heart away from sin. A Bible in the hands is of great value, but a Bible in a heart is of much greater value. Hide the Word of God in your heart. Obviously, that would involve memorizing it. This also involves knowing it; tuck God's Word away in your heart. Know what He says about Himself and His home. Know what He says about salvation—know it well. Know what He says about sin and the world. Know what He says about relationships, marriage, and family. Know what He says about money and valuables. Know what He says about being part of the body of Christ. Know what He says about the tongue. Know what He says about trials and temptation. Know what He says about winning the lost. Hide it in your heart.

Meditate on it.

> *But his delight is in the law of the LORD; and in his law doth he meditate day and night.* Psalm 1:2

I am reminded of the time my husband and I were engaged. During that time we were together a lot, and we were apart a lot. But whether we were together or not, I was thinking about him. When I worked, I thought about him. When I was with friends, I thought about him. As I drifted off to sleep, I thought about him. Day and night, I thought about him. That type of consuming thought should be given to the Word of God. Ponder it. Feed on it. Read it, study it, look intently at it, and meditate on it. Read passages over and over again until you understand them and you know them well. Use tools such as a Bible dictionary and concordance to help you in your study. Take notes as you read to help you remember the things you learn. Be consumed with knowing God's Word.

Delight in it.
When you believe that the Bible is the key to success in your

life both now and in the future, you will develop a love for it. Value the Word of God. Delight in it. While it is true you can decide to take pleasure in the Bible, delight will most naturally come as you learn it and apply it. Your love for it will grow as you see the truths come to life in your life. Your delight will become more intense as you observe God's promises come to pass. You will not delight in something you never take time with. Spend time with the Word of God. As you do, you will be able to say as the psalmist:

> *O how love I thy law!...How sweet are thy words unto my taste! yea, sweeter than honey to my mouth.*
> Psalm 119:97a, 103

Do It!

The instruction label for the red sheets said, "Wash separately in warm water." I had done that several times and assumed that all the loose dye was long gone. Since there was a pile of laundry, it would save time to wash a few other things in the same load as those sheets. So I threw in a few of my son's favorite stuffed animals. You guessed it. They all turned pink. Oh, I was so upset at myself. (And my son was plenty upset too!) I knew what the instructions said. I even knew why they gave me that warning. But I did not follow it. I was foolish on that day. And any one who hears and knows the instruction of God, but does not follow it, is foolish as well.

But be ye doers of the word, and not hearers only, deceiving your own selves. For if any be a hearer of the word, and not a doer, he is like unto a man beholding his natural face in a glass: For he beholdeth himself, and goeth his way, and straightway forgetteth what manner of man he was. But whoso looketh into the perfect law of liberty, and continueth therein, he being not a forgetful hearer, but a doer of the work, this man shall be blessed in his deed. James 1:22-25

The reason you spend time in front of your mirror each morning is to see what needs to be corrected. What if you stood for a minute staring at your image and saw your hair standing up in several different directions? You saw that you had small pieces of your breakfast still in your teeth. You saw little flecks of dirt in the corners of your eyes. You saw that your shirt was badly wrinkled and had a stain on the collar. Then you walked out the door and headed to school. What good would that minute's look in the mirror be? It would have given you knowledge of the problems that existed; but, past that, there would be no profit. The purpose of the mirror is to show you things that need fixing so that you can fix them. While it is good for you to know the rules and principles of life God has given in His Word, that knowledge is of little profit to you if you do not do what it says. The rules of a game are of little value when the players decide to play their own way. The washing instructions on red sheets are of little value when the person washing decides to do it differently. Perhaps the tag should have included the warning: you no makka the sheets, you no makka the instructions. You did not create the world and the things in it including yourself. The One Who gives life is the One Who knows how it should go. And that wonderful

Creator gave us an instruction book. Its guidance, however, will help only as you obey it. Read the Bible. Hear the Bible preached. Know the Bible. But don't leave off the most important part—do it!

JOURNAL THOUGHTS

❑   I have not been reading the Bible but am making the decision to begin making Bible reading a habit in my life.

❑   I have been reading the Bible but see that I could make that time more profitable in these ways:

❑   I have not been taking advantage of hearing the preaching of God's Word as frequently as I should and am making the decision to go hear it as often as possible.

❑   I have not gotten full help from the preaching that I hear because I have not been listening, have not made decisions, or have not asked for extra help. I am making the decision to get the most out of preaching by doing these things:

* NOTE: Sharing the decisions you make in this book with someone you trust would also be a wise way to get as much help as you can. Who can you share these decisions with?

❑   I realize that I need to know the Bible better and am making a decision to increase my knowledge by:

❑   I have not been doing what I know the Bible says and am making a decision to obey it in these areas:

CHAPTER FOUR

That's Not Fair — I Cheated!

Isn't it maddening when you are playing a game and someone cheats? Do you remember playing hide and seek as a kid? The leader of the gang sets the boundaries. You can hide in the front yard, back yard, neighbor's yard, and in the lot across the street. But you cannot hide inside the house or in the shed. Everyone agrees. You play for a while, and then it is your turn to count: "1, 2, 3…20. Ready or not, here I come." You look and look and look, but you just cannot find that one person. Eventually, you discover that he is hiding in the shed. Oh, it makes you so mad, and you say, "That's not fair! You cheated!" You are so angry, in fact, that you refuse to play the game anymore and stomp your way home.

Most of the time, anger is wrong. Being angry at the cheater is wrong. In Ephesians 4:26 and 27, however, God gives us a time when not only is it all right to be mad, but He encourages us to be so.

> *Be ye angry, and sin not: let not the sun go down upon your wrath: Neither give place to the devil.* Ephesians 4:26-27

At a quick glance you might think that this verse is telling us that we should never go to bed angry. Many married couples follow that rule in their homes. While it is a good rule, its basis is not from this passage. This verse says: *Be ye angry.* It does not say: Do *not* be angry. It seems odd that God would tell us that He wants us to be mad, until you realize that He wants us to be mad at our sin. Be angry; be angry; be angry. Do not let the sun go down on that anger. In other words, always be angry about sin. If you let up on your anger toward sin, you are giving room for the devil to come in and defeat you. This verse is so powerful in that it gives us a key to open the door of victory in the Christian life. Be angry at sin.

The rest of the chapter makes it clear that not only are we to be angry at sin in a general sense, but we should also be furious with our own sin. It mentions several sins that we should put away: lying, stealing, corrupt communication, bitterness, wrath, anger, clamour, evil speaking, and anything which is corrupt. Be angry at sin. Be angry about your sin. As mad as you might have been at the neighbor kid for cheating, it should scarcely compare to your anger toward your sin. You should be filled with a righteous anger that says, "That's not fair, *I* cheated!"

A Big, Ugly, Hairy Spider

Christianity in general is stirred up about sin. It angers us to hear of the wickedness that takes place every day around the world. We have no trouble being mad at horrific sins that take place in our country. But rarely do we think about our own sin. We excuse things that seem little. We allow our mouths to speak unkindness and do not give it a second thought. We harbor bitterness or pride in our hearts with no regret. We allow wicked scenes to pass before our eyes and feed wicked thoughts. We live seeking to please ourselves. We easily follow the crowd and talk about how hard it is to stand up for what is right. We excuse our rebellion toward authority by claiming authority is unfair. We compare our lives with those around us instead of comparing our lives with the perfect God. In doing so we feel we are okay.

During my freshman year of college I learned a lot about comparing myself to others. Christian college was such a new experience for me. It was awesome to be around hundreds of other believers. I met a girl early in the first semester that obviously knew more of the Bible than I. I thought she would be a good friend, and that I could learn a lot from her. On Saturdays, we would go shopping together with a couple other friends. As soon as we drove off the campus, she would turn on the radio to a rock station. I thought it was a little unusual, but convinced myself it must be all right because these were good Christian girls. They had so much more experience in living the Christian life than I; surely they would not do something wrong. I compared myself to them. Since every day I heard preaching in chapel and teaching in Bible classes, it did not take long to realize that I was wrong. They were wrong. I quickly found some new friends. Only God and His Word should be the standard for comparison. When we compare ourselves to His Word, our sin is revealed. That sin ought to make us furious.

Evangelist Cranston Knowles pointed out a girl in the crowd of listeners during one of his preaching services. He had us imagine there was a spider crawling up her back. She cannot see it, but as it reaches her shoulder a friend notices it and says to her, "Don't move." Well, of course, the girl's eyes follow the eyes of her friend and she spots the spider. Immediately she goes in panic mode. Aughhhhhhhh! She frantically swipes and bats at that spider until it is gone. Evangelist Knowles then explained that this same panic mode should be our response to sin.

> *Let love be without dissimulation. Abhor that which is evil; cleave to that which is good.* Romans 12:9

Just as we detest a spider, so we ought to detest evil. That message was such a help to me. Several times since, when I was confronted by God about my sin, I could picture that sin sitting on my shoulder just like an ugly spider. Mentally I have frantically swiped at it. That type of hatred toward sin can change a life. You will never get serious about living right if you do not hate living wrong. If you do not despise your sin, it will begin to set up house on your shoulder and invite over friends. You will not even be able to see that ugly thing sitting there. There is nothing threatening it. It is comfortable there. But if, with eyes full of anger, you turn your head and see it, then that sin-spider is in trouble.

The time to begin practicing hatred of sin is now. It is such an important part of being prepared for the future. If you have many ugly, hairy spiders living on your shoulder, you are going to be weighed down. Had you not been furious with the cheater, you would have continued to play the game. In the same way, if you are not angry at your sin, you will continue to have it and even love it. You will not possibly be able to do what God wants you to do – now or later.

Recognizing Spiders

Sunday morning after the service, the pastor of the church we were visiting took us out to eat at a cafeteria-style restaurant. Due to the long line of people behind us and a hungry baby in my arms, I felt rushed to choose the items I wanted. I glanced quickly at the options and pointed to a gravy-covered Salisbury steak and several side items. The servers piled the food on and handed me my plate. I then followed the rest of the group to our table. We thanked God for the meal and began to eat. One bite and I realized that what I had picked was not Salisbury steak but liver. I hate liver! And now I had to figure out what to do with the pile of it on my plate.

The reason I ended up with liver is not because I forgot I hated it, but because I did not recognize it. Do you hate your sin? Are you convinced that you need a righteous anger toward it? That is so important. Now you need to learn to recognize it, or else it will be plopped on your plate of life without your realizing it. The most repulsive spider can ride around on your shoulder for a long time if you do not know it is there. Learn to see the spiders. Recognize your sin.

Know the Word of God.

The Bible is essential. You will not recognize sin apart from it.

> *What shall we say then? Is the law sin? God forbid. Nay, I had not known sin, but by the law: for I had not known lust, except the law had said, Thou shalt not covet....Wherefore the law is holy, and the commandment holy, and just, and good. Was then that which is good made death unto me? God forbid. But sin, that it might appear sin, working death in me by that which is good; that sin by the commandment might become exceeding sinful.* Romans 7:7, 12-13

Without the law, without the Word of God, none of us would know what sin is. We would be hopelessly lost but never know it. You know that it is wrong to murder. How do you know it? The answer is the law. God said it is sin. Paul says here that the law pointed out sin. And in seeing sin, he could see that he was guilty of it. And in seeing that he was guilty of it, he could then see his need for a Savior. Without the Word of God, we would never know sin and thereby never know salvation.

If the Bible is the key to knowing sin in order that we may know salvation, would it not also make sense that the Bible is the key to knowing how to live *after* salvation? It is. We cannot possibly know what pleases and displeases God apart from His Word.

Wherewithal shall a young man cleanse his way? by taking heed thereto according to thy word. With my whole heart have I sought thee: O let me not wander from thy commandments. Thy word have I hid in mine heart, that I might not sin against thee. Psalm 119:9-11

Here we see that it is important for a Christian to memorize Scriptures, to learn what God says and meditate on it in the heart. Then the Word of God, hidden in the heart, comes to the conscience in time of stress and temptation and reminds one, "Don't do that! That is a sin." (When a Christian Sins, John R. Rice, pg. 112)

You must go time and time again to the Bible. (I hope this is sounding familiar!) Read it. Learn it. Study it. Memorize it. Hear it preached. If you fail to do so, you will have liver on your plate and spiders on your shoulder.

Judge yourself.

Take time each day to examine yourself. Reflect on your conversations, your actions, your thoughts, and your attitudes. Were there any words you spoke that were unkind, complaining, or perverse? Did you think nasty things about your parents, your teacher, or your friends? Did you allow your mind to wander into wicked imaginations? Did you worry? Were you sarcastic in your comments toward authority? Did you watch something that was worldly? The point is that you need to judge yourself by God's Word daily.

For if we would judge ourselves, we should not be judged.
I Corinthians 11:31

While this verse is specifically dealing with preparing oneself for the Lord's Supper, it certainly applies anytime—all the time. So many Christians take little or no time to examine themselves. It is no wonder they cannot see the spiders sitting on their shoulders since they seldom look there.

The heart is deceitful above all things, and desperately wicked: who can know it? Jeremiah 17:9

We are blinded to our own wickedness; it is greater than we could ever imagine. When a person examines herself in light of the Word of God, asking God to open her blind eyes, sin will surface. How can you hate something that has not surfaced—that you do not even know about? Look for the spiders. Assume that they are there.

Fleeing Spiders

Abstain from all appearance of evil. 1 Thessalonians 5:22

A prudent man forseeth the evil, and hideth himself: but the simple pass on, and are punished. Proverbs 22:3

Remove thy way far from her, and come not nigh the door of her house. Proverbs 5:8

Flee sin. Do not allow yourself to get anywhere near it. Be

as Joseph who, when tempted by Potiphar's wife, fled. He ran away. He got as far from that temptation as he could. He avoided it.

I have a friend who was an alcoholic. She was saved and has had victory in that area. She has told me, however, that it is hard. It is a great temptation day in and day out for her. What a challenge every time she sees or especially smells alcohol — almost an unbearable challenge! Would it not be foolish of her to walk by a bar or night club when the smell of the booze permeates all the surrounding area? Would it not be crazy of her to go to a neighbor's backyard BBQ when she knows beer will be available there? She has to remove herself far from it. She needs to foresee the evil and hide herself from it. We need to do the same. Whether it be alcohol, immorality, pride, worldly entertainment, rebellion, materialism — flee from it. Avoid all of it. Hide from it.

I grew up with a lot of television. My parents did not watch much, but I watched all the time. I was so hardened to the sin that came across the screen that it rarely bothered me. I did not realize that sin was permeating my mind because of it. In college, however, I could not watch television. It was not permitted. The absence of it was one of the best things that happened in my college days. I became convinced that most of it was wicked and that, furthermore, I had been addicted to it. When my husband and I married, we made a decision to foresee the evil and hide from it. We chose not to have a television in our home. It is easy to see what a wise decision that was for us whenever we spend the night in a motel. That TV is there. We often have checked to see if there is anything good on. And before long we have watched far more than we should have. The temptation of television, even after all these years, is great for both of us. How foolish it would be to have one in our home! How foolish it is to allow ourselves to channel surf while staying at motels.

Are you fleeing from sin? Maybe you need to get a TV out of your room. Maybe you need to get rid of some books or magazines. Maybe you need to flee from some friends. Maybe you need to end a relationship. Are you foreseeing the evil and hiding from it, or are you knocking on its door? Are you swiping away the spiders, or are you inviting them to come a little closer? Stay as far away from temptation as you can.

Eliminating Spiders

It can be a horrifying thing to turn and see a spider crawling around on your shoulder. In the same way, it can seem hopeless when you realize you have sinned. While it is true that sin is horrific and wicked, Jesus Christ has given us the opportunity to have it removed immediately. Though our fellowship with God has been broken, it can be restored. The promise to believers of I John 1:9 tells us how.

> *If we confess our sins, he is faithful and just to forgive us our sins, and to cleanse us from all unrighteousness.* I John 1:9

Confess means "to say the same thing as." To confess our sin to God is to say the same thing about that sin as He does — to say that it is sin. So if I have lied and broken my fellowship with God, I need to eliminate that spider by confessing it. Confession is not admitting I made a little mistake and will try to do better next time. Confession is calling that mistake what it is – sin. "Father, I lied. Lying is sin. In doing so, I sinned against you." The promise here is that God will forgive you and cleanse you. Listen to David's confession after he committed adultery and murder.

Have mercy upon me, O God, according to thy lovingkindness: according unto the multitude of thy tender mercies blot out my transgressions. Wash me throughly from mine iniquity, and cleanse me from my sin. For I acknowledge my transgressions: and my sin is ever before me. Against thee, thee only, have I sinned, and done this evil in thy sight: that thou mightest be justified when thou speakest, and be clear when thou judgest.... Purge me with hyssop, and I shall be clean: wash me, and I shall be whiter than snow....Hide thy face from my sins, and blot out all mine iniquities. Create in me a clean heart, O God; and renew a right spirit within me. Psalm 51:1-4, 7, 9-10

Some years later David's son Solomon wrote:

He that covereth his sins shall not prosper: but whoso confesseth and forsaketh them shall have mercy.
Proverbs 28:13

You can have mercy. You can have forgiveness. Every time. That spider can be eliminated and should be.

The Hate of Chrysostom

Oh, how we should hate sin! It is said that when the emperor of Constantinople arrested Chrysostom and thought of trying to make him recant, the great preacher slowly shook his head. The emperor said to his attendants, "Put him in prison."

"No," said one of them, "he will be glad to go because he delights in the presence of his God in quiet."

"Well, then let us execute him," said the emperor.

"He will be glad to die," said the attendant, "for he wants to go to heaven. I heard him say so the other day. There is only one thing that can give Chrysostom pain, and that is to make him sin; he said he was afraid of nothing but sin. If you make him sin, you will make him unhappy."

Christians should fear sin like that and hate sin like that! God hates sin, and we must hate it too. (When a Christian Sins, John R. Rice, pp. 70-71)

JOURNAL THOUGHTS

❑   I have not been angry at the sin in my life but now see the need to hate my sin.

❑   I need to take these steps to help my recognition of sin:

❑   I see the need to flee from these sins that are a temptation to me:

❑   This is the plan of action that I need to take in order to stay away from/flee specific sin temptations:

❑   I have unconfessed sin in my life and am making the decision to confess these specific things to Him:

CHAPTER FIVE

Surrender, Seek and Find

Since it was the fall of my senior year, I needed to think about college. I had attended public school all my life, and I knew that I did not want to go a secular college. I wanted to go to a Christian college. That was all I knew. I did not know the names of Christian colleges. I did not know where any were, and I did not know anything about them. But I knew God wanted me at one, and I wanted to go to the right one for me. I was a very immature Christian. I knew very little of the Bible, and I knew very few people who could be a help to me. But since I did want God's will, I sought Him about it. My prayers were simple, asking God to show me the right place to go. I had no way of finding out by myself. I had no one to tell me what to do. I was in desperate need of God's leading.

I feel confident that God was thrilled to give me that direction. He provided the miracle answer I needed. There was a lot to overcome. God certainly was not pleased that

I was such an immature believer or that I knew little of His Word. But He saw my heart of surrender to His will and heard my prayers asking for His leading. He kept true to His promises that, at the time, I did not even know. There have been many times since then that I have needed to know God's will for my life. In some cases I sought His leading fully surrendered. Other times I have foolishly trusted my own instincts and plans. My goal is to know and obey God's will in every area of my life. It is my prayer that you will make that your own goal as well.

God's Will — For What?

Many young people and adults alike have the notion that finding God's will only applies to teens or those in their early twenties. After all, they think, it is at that age when one needs to know what to do with the rest of her life. It is true that there are some big decisions that will be made during that stage of life, and it is so important that those decisions line up with what God wants. But God's will for your life is not limited to those few decisions. Do not be duped into thinking that. Certainly, you need to know God's will about college, marriage and your career. But you also need to know God's will in every decision you make today and tomorrow.

I have graduated from college, married, and been led into a ministry. Those are decisions of the past for me, yet I need God's leading and knowledge of His will as much now as I did years ago before those decisions were made. My young daughter is in as much need of doing God's will now as she will be in later years. What class should you take? When should you get married? What should you do this Saturday? Which dress should you buy? How much offering should you give this week? What should you study in college? Should you go to camp this summer? Should you watch that movie? Should you apply for that job? Should you join the choir? It does not matter if the decision seems huge or small; God has a will for you. He wants you to choose what He wants for you. He wants you to seek Him in all those decisions. He wants to be involved in every area of your life. The principles of surrender, seeking and finding apply no matter how old you are or what decision you are facing.

Surrender

Finding God's will in any decision demands surrender. I can remember a time when my heart's desire was for God's will in my life—or at least I thought it was. But God was showing me that He wanted me to make a change in my life that I did not like. I wrestled with the issue for quite a while, even convincing myself that it was Satan who was telling me to do what I did not want to do. Deep in my heart I knew it was God. But I would not surrender to it. I would not obey God. I would not do His will. And I jeopardized much of my future because I wanted *my* way. I thought what God wanted could not possibly be the best in that situation. God's way was too hard. I was not truly surrendered to Him. Thankfully, God continued to work in my life. I eventually submitted to His will and later could easily see how it was best.

When you are seeking to know what to do, when you want to know what direction to head, when you desire to follow the Lord's leading—you must surrender your thoughts, your desires, your plans, and your way to him. You must be willing to follow when God leads. Maybe you would be quick to say, "I am surrendered to God's will." I am quick to say that too when God's will is easy, when I agree, and when I can see that it is the best. Yet when God directs in a way that is not easy, in a way that offends the flesh, in a way that does not make sense—we can find that perhaps we are not as surrendered as we first supposed.

> *I beseech you therefore, brethren, by the mercies of God, that ye present your bodies a living sacrifice, holy, acceptable unto God, which is your reasonable service.* Romans 12:1

Here Paul is encouraging believers to present their lives to God as a sacrifice. To sacrifice something is to give it up— fully. To sacrifice your life to God is to give it up—fully. It is to make a decision to keep your hands off it. It means surrendering it. It is to say, "Not my will, Lord, but Yours." That involves your future. That involves today. It involves big decisions and little ones. In order to live in God's will, you must have every part of your life surrendered.

Many young women struggle with God's will when they see themselves having passed the age when most get married. They have what is sometimes called "senior panic." They are soon to graduate from college and have not yet met their future husband. In their minds, time has run out, and they are despondent. Maybe they do not say it, but it is obvious they are battling with God. "What if I never get married? What is God doing here? All my friends are engaged, and I have no one." They refuse to rest in God's will. They refuse to believe that what He has for them is best. Often they begin to act foolishly around young men because of this desperation. They flirt, they hint, they chase. In doing so, they drive away all of the guys around them. I have been around several young single men who have said they would not go anywhere near a particular girl simply because she was obviously trying to find a husband. Her lack of surrender to God not only causes her turmoil but also hinders her from being in the position to meet the man God would have for her. These young women need to remember that their lives are God's business. Single or married—have you presented your body a living sacrifice? Then, of course, God has a right to direct in your life, whether it be about marriage or any other area. And He has the right to tell you what to do. If you have given yourself to Him, do what He says and go where He leads.

The life of the prophet is beautiful in Isaiah 6:8. God speaks to Isaiah telling him that there is a job that needs to be done saying, *"Whom shall I send, and who will go for us?"* Isaiah answers, *"Here am I."* Those three words speak volumes about Isaiah. Isaiah was presenting his body a living sacrifice to God. Here am I, God. I am yours. You can do whatever you want with me. I am not my own. I belong to you. Then Isaiah says, *"Send me."* After he acknowledges that his life is not his own, Isaiah asks God to let him do the job. "I will do what you want done, Lord. You need a man to do your work — let me be the one." God had not yet laid out the specifics of the job. He did not give all the details first and then ask who would do it. He simply said that He had a job that needed to be done. Isaiah did not say, "What is the job, Lord? Perhaps it is something I will want to do." No, Isaiah said, *"Here am I; send me."* Then God told him what to do. At that point Isaiah did not have to decide whether he would do the job or not; the decision had already been made.

When you view every part of your life as a sacrifice, when every decision becomes God's, when you acknowledge that you have no rights, when you realize that you are not your own — then God's will becomes very real. It is not so much a battle. Peace and joy become yours. Your life becomes exactly what God wants it to be; and there is no life better than that!

Seek

After your life is surrendered, you need to seek God's will for today and tomorrow. You need to seek God's will in small decisions and large ones. In the process of seeking His will, you need to become convinced of several biblical truths and promises.

God's will never contradicts His Word.
The easiest place to find and know God's will is in His Word. He wrote the Bible so that we would know Him and His desires for our lives. Since it is His will for all men to be

saved, He explains in the Bible how to be saved. It is His will for all believers to live holy, separated lives. He states that many times in His Word. He has a will concerning marriage, rearing children, finances, authorities, churches, clothing, relationships and much more. These are all revealed in the Bible. Your knowing God's will in any area of your life has a direct relationship to your knowing God's Word. The more you know of His Word, the more you will know His will. The more you read and study His Word, the more you will see His heart. The more you see His heart, the more you will know His will for you.

God says in the Bible that He never changes and neither does His Word. Therefore, it is always reliable. What the Bible says is always God's will. God will never lead you to do something that is the opposite of His Word. King Saul learned this lesson when God told him to go and conquer the Amalekites and to destroy all of them and all that they had. Saul went to battle and did destroy all the Amalekites, except for the king and the best of the animals. King Saul saved those to sacrifice to God. When God sent the prophet Samuel to confront him, Saul said, *"Blessed be thou of the LORD: I have performed the commandment of the LORD"* (I Samuel 15:13b). Samuel then asked Saul about the animals:

> *And Saul said, They have brought them from the Amalekites: for the people spared the best of the sheep and of the oxen, to sacrifice unto the LORD thy God; and the rest we have utterly destroyed....Yea, I have obeyed the voice of the LORD, and have gone the way which the LORD sent me, and have brought Agag the king of Amalek, and have utterly destroyed*

the Amalekites. But the people took of the spoil, sheep and oxen, the chief of the things which should have been utterly destroyed, to sacrifice unto the LORD thy God in Gilgal. I Samuel 15:15, 20-21

King Saul was certain that God would be pleased. He destroyed the Amalekites and saved a few of the best sheep and oxen to sacrifice to God. Surely God would honor their sacrifice. But God said through Samuel:

Hath the LORD as great delight in burnt offerings and sacrifices, as in obeying the voice of the LORD? Behold, to obey is better than sacrifice, and to hearken than the fat of rams. I Samuel 15:22

You see, King Saul thought he knew God's will was to save a few animals for sacrifice. But God had given His Word and therefore had made known His will. All was to be destroyed. It is a great temptation to do what we think God wants us to do when that very thing is opposed to His Word. God's will never contradicts His Word.

There is a young lady who has dated an unsaved young man for a while. The man proposes, and she is left to decide if she ought to marry him. She prays and seeks God's leading and feels that God told her that, yes, she should go ahead and marry him. She feels confident that if this man were her husband she would be able to see him saved. In her seeking of God's will, however, she has failed to remember that God will never contradict His Word. The Bible is clear that a believer should not be yoked together with an unbeliever.

That yoke or bond could apply to several relationships, certainly one of which is marriage. It is not God's desire for her to marry the unsaved man. God's Word is always supreme. It needs to be supreme over our feelings, our thoughts, our desires, and our search for God's will. If we think that God's leading in our lives does contradict His Word, we need to follow His Word. To obey is better than sacrifice.

God's will is obedience to parents.

Children, obey your parents in the Lord: for this is right. Honour thy father and mother; which is the first commandment with promise. Ephesians 6:1-2

Honour thy father and thy mother: that thy days may be long upon the land which the LORD thy God giveth thee. Exodus 20:12

My son, keep thy father's commandment, and forsake not the law of thy mother. Proverbs 6:20

A child who is still in the home, whether she is one, six, eighteen, or twenty-one, is under the authority of her parents. When she marries, then that authority changes hands. Until that time, she is to obey her parents. Many conflicts arise when young women want to have their own way and refuse to obey their parents. It is *always* God's will for a child still in the home to obey her parents. Remember, God's will is supreme. It does not matter if you like what your parents say, if you think their direction is wise, or if it makes sense to you. **You are not in God's will if you are not obeying Dad and Mom.**

When I was seeking God about where to go to college, I had great freedom from my parents in the decision. They left it up to me. There was only one thing my father asked of me. He knew I had my heart set on going to a Christian college but wanted me to visit at least one secular college before making a final decision. It would have been easy to rebel and fuss at him about it. But my primary job was to obey my parents. And so, when I picked out a secular college a few hours away, we went to see it. To refuse to go would have been out of God's will. God's will for me was to visit that college because God's will for me was to obey my parents.

The question you may have in your mind is this: "What if my parents tell me to do something that is wrong?" It is a legitimate question. However, many of the young people who ask this question are not so much interested in really knowing the answer as they are in verbalizing their rebellion. One who quickly puts up that wall of defense is one whose life is characterized by disobedience. She will fuss, whine, complain, roll her eyes, and rebel against the rules of the home. She does not really care to know what the Bible says about the answer. She just wants her own way and, as long as she remains in that rebellion, will never be in the will of God. But the Bible does have an answer to that question.

> *Children, obey your parents <u>in all things</u>: for this is well pleasing unto the Lord.* Colossians 3:20

God says you are to obey in all things. It may be hard to believe or hard to swallow, but, according to Colossians 3:20, you are to obey even if you are told to do something you think is wrong. Now, if you do so properly and meekly, I do believe you have the liberty to make an appeal to your parents' decision. Suppose your parents want you to go to a Hollywood movie, and you think it is wrong. Kindly, gently, and with a submissive spirit you could say, "Mom, you know that I try to obey God, and He says in his Word that we should not put anything wicked before our eyes. I would really rather not go to the movies tonight, but I will do whatever you decide." Many times God intervenes and makes a way of escape for the submissive believer.

The same is true in a husband and wife relationship. Learning submission to your parents now will help you in future relationships. If you rebel against Mom and Dad, then you will most likely rebel against your husband's leadership someday as well. And the Bible also clearly states that a wife is to submit to her husband.

> *For after this manner in the old time the holy women also, who trusted in God, adorned themselves, being in subjection unto their own husbands: Even as Sara obeyed Abraham, calling him lord: whose daughters ye are, as long as ye do well, and are not afraid with any amazement.* I Peter 3:5-6

Sarah was a beautiful woman. So beautiful, in fact, that Abraham was afraid for his life because of her. Abraham was convinced that the King of Gerar would kill him and take Sarah as his own wife. So Abraham told Sarah to lie about being his wife. The Bible does not record the conversation that may have taken place between Abraham and Sarah. But I can imagine it might have been a little like this: "Sarah, the king will see your beauty and kill me for it. So we must not tell him that you are my wife. Instead, we will tell him that you are my sister."

Sarah, who the Bible tells us was submissive, even calling her husband lord, may have appealed saying, "My Husband, allow me to speak. What you are asking me to do is to lie— to sin against God. This king will surely take me as his wife if he thinks I have no other husband. I am afraid great evil will come upon us if we do this."

"But, Sarah, we will not be lying. You are my half-sister. Do you want me to be killed? Will that be better for you? No, this is the plan, and that is what you will do." Sarah obeyed—even when she was told to do something that was wrong.

It is easy to think what an awful thing that was and that surely God should not have expected Sarah to be submissive to her husband in that situation. But what a wonderful end to the story that can teach us so much about our God! Abraham and Sarah did lie to the king, and the king did take Sarah. But God told that king in a dream that if he touched Sarah he would die, because she was another man's wife. The next morning the king confronted Abraham.

> *What hast thou done unto us? and what have I offended thee,*
> *that thou hast brought on me and on my kingdom a great sin?*

thou hast done deeds unto me that ought not to be done. And Abimelech…restored him Sarah his wife. Genesis 20:9b, 14

Not only did the king rebuke Abraham for his wrong, but he showed that Sarah was not to be blamed.

And unto Sarah he said, Behold, I have given thy brother a thousand pieces of silver; behold, he is to thee a covering of the eyes, unto all that are with thee, and with all other: thus she was reproved. Genesis 20:16

Reproved here means cleared. The king righted the wrong done *to* Sarah. Even the king knew that Sarah was not to be blamed. She was right in obeying her husband. This Sarah who was taken by a king is the same Sarah that the Bible tells wives to be like. We should follow her example of submission.

The God of Sarah is your God as well. Can He not perform miracles in your situation? But first you must do what is right and obey.

A young man in Christian college told me about his high school years, most of which were spent in public school. He wished that he could be homeschooled or attend a Christian school, but he had no choice in the matter. His parents made the decision. He mentioned that there were challenges to living a godly life in that situation, but it helped so much to know he was in God's will. He was resting in the fact that his job was to honor his parents. That assurance, he said, gave him needed confidence to live right in a wicked place.

He was a good testimony in that school in part because he understood that God's will is obedience to parents.

God's will is revealed as I obey step by step.

It is no wonder that many people do not know what to do when they come to a major decision in their lives. They feel like they have no way of finding out what God wants them to do. They seem to walk about in darkness. That happens because, when God did lead in the past, they did not obey. When they were confronted with sin, they ignored the conviction. They rebelled against the preaching they heard. They rebelled against the help they received from their parents and church leaders. They refused to do God's will day in and day out. They went their own way. And now they are crying out to God wondering why they cannot hear His answer. They do not know the voice of God; they do not know how to hear it because they have rejected it time and time again. God is ready to forgive. God wants to answer. But if you refuse to obey in what He is showing you today, you can have no assurance of His will later in your life. I have read the story of a woman who was seeking God in a particular need; and every time she went to pray, God pointed out a sin that she had yet to make right. Eventually, she realized that God would not give her the help that she needed until she obeyed Him in this other matter.

Many young women seek God about finding a mate. "Oh, Lord, please bring the right man into my life and help me to know who is right." But these same women refuse to submit to God when He shows them that they have been living in sin. They have been involved physically with

men who are not their husbands. Yet they expect to know
God's will concerning their future. God's will is revealed
as I am obedient—step by step—each time He leads me.
Obedience today greatly affects the future. If you want to
have confidence that you will have God's leading in the
future, follow his leading for today.

God's will can be found through prayer.

Are you not sure what to do? Ask God. Remember my story
about searching for a college? I had no idea what college
was God's will for me. I was surrendered. I knew going to
a Christian college matched up with the Bible. I obeyed my
parents about it. But I still needed direction from God. So I
asked. I prayed and begged God to show me His will.

You can ask God to show you His will about anything. If you
do not know if the Bible says anything about your need, ask
God to show you where in His Word you can get help. Ask
your parents or church leaders if they know any verses that
give guidance to your need. If you know the Bible does not
give you the specific direction you need, ask God to show
you His will. Do not spend your time worrying about it.
Pray. God wants you to come to Him and seek His leading.
He wants you to have it. He is not sitting in heaven laughing
at you because He wants to make you figure this one out on
your own. He wants you to admit that you need Him.

> *If any of you lack wisdom, let him ask of God, that giveth to all
> men liberally, and upbraideth not; and it shall be given him.*
> James 1:5

Needing to know God's will in any situation certainly qualifies as lacking wisdom. This verse and the ones following promise that, if you ask in faith for the wisdom that you need, God will answer. Do you need to know what is right? Do you need to know what to do? Do you need to know where to go? Do you need to know how to handle a problem? Do you need to know what to say? ASK!

Find

Perhaps the most encouraging and easiest verses to understand about knowing God's will are in Proverbs 3.

> *Trust in the LORD with all thine heart; and lean not unto thine own understanding. In all thy ways acknowledge him, and he shall direct thy paths. Be not wise in thine own eyes: fear the LORD, and depart from evil.* Proverbs 3:5-7

You can easily see the need for surrender here. Acknowledge God; do not depend on what you think. Do not assume you know what is best. *Be not wise in thine own eyes.* You can also see the need for obedience to God's Word which includes obedience to you parents. *Fear the LORD, and depart from evil.* A person who fears God does what He says. Trusting in God implies that you have sought Him with your need. The best part is that you can have the promise of finding direction. *And he shall direct thy paths.* He will show you. He will lead you. You can claim that promise. Rest assured that God will direct your path.

JOURNAL THOUGHTS

❑ I have never presented myself as a sacrifice to God and am making that decision today. I want to do His will in every area of my life.

DATE:_____

—OR—

❑ I have already presented myself a sacrifice to God, but have not been living in light of that decision. I need to submit to God's leading in these areas:

❑ I have been seeking God's will without His Word. I need to find out and submit to what the Bible says about:

❑ I realize that to live in God's will I must obey my parents.

❑   I have sinned in my rebellion against them in these ways:

❑   I have been asking for God's will but ignoring these sins in my life:

❑   I have not been asking for God's leading concerning:

❑   I am claiming the promise that God will direct me in His will concerning:

CHAPTER SIX
Dogs and Vacuum Cleaners

I love dogs. There is something about being with a dog that lightens my heart. When the neighbor's dog wanders over to my yard for a pat on the head, I am thrilled. I look forward to the times when a friend asks our family to keep his dog while he is away. I love petting dogs. I enjoy playing with them. I get a kick out of just looking at them. During most of my childhood, I had a dog. But I distinctly remember a time when I did not. Buffy, the dog my family got before I was born, had died. Crackers, the dog we had kept for over a year while my aunt and uncle were overseas, had gone back home. I was in Junior High and I was dog-less. I felt empty. There was no friendly slurp to greet me when I came home from school. There was no wagging tail, flopping ears, or clinking collar. I missed the entertainment of watching a furry friend try to get peanut butter off the roof of his mouth. How I wanted a dog! Finally, after weeks turned into months and I felt I could not bear it any longer, I brought up the subject. "I need a dog," I blurted out to my parents fully expecting to have my hopes dashed forever. But instead, only a short time later, we were out shopping for one. Before I knew it, I had Bandit. I never dreamed it could be that easy. If only I had known, I would have asked a lot sooner.

A lady I know had an old vacuum—a really old vacuum. How she tired of trying to use that heavy machine that did not work well! It frustrated her day after day, but she did not have the money to spend on a new one. Time passed on and on as she wrestled with the clunky thing. One day as she was convicted by the Word of God about the importance of prayer, she decided to ask God for a different vacuum. It was not long before a brand new one landed in her home. I imagine after the initial excitement wore off she felt like kicking herself wondering why she did not ask for one sooner.

I was frustrated because I had blown it in a conversation with a friend. I had been guilty of saying some things that I should not have. I had not set a watch on my tongue. Before the next conversation, I asked God to give me wisdom and keep my tongue from uttering anything it should not utter. And He directed me to guard my speech. If only I had asked for help in the previous conversation.

How many blessings do we miss out on because we do not ask for them? How often is help available to us that we do not receive because we do not ask for it? How many needs go unmet because we do not ask? If we truly knew the answers to these questions, I suspect we would all kick ourselves for not asking. Asking God for help, for the things we need every day, for the desires of our hearts sounds like such an easy thing to do. Yet we can let days and weeks pass without uttering a prayer. You see, while praying can be so simple and easy, it is also one of the most difficult challenges of the Christian life.

So Easy!

It is easy because it does not require strenuous physical exertion. In fact there are scores of things we do each day that are more physically demanding. It is easy because it is not limited by location or tool. Friends of ours were going through trying days filled with medical testing. We wanted to be a help to them by watching their several children. But when the biopsies were finally scheduled, we were out of town. We felt frustrated and helpless. We had wanted to help; we had planned to help. But we were in the wrong place when the time of need came. That never happens with prayer. You can pray anywhere and in any situation. Prayer is easy because you do not need anyone else to do it. There are definite benefits to praying with others, but it is not required. You can pray alone — even without uttering an audible word. You do not need someone seemingly more spiritual to ask God for you. You can go to God yourself. Prayer is easy because it does not require you to know and understand everything about it before you begin. While learning all you can will help mature your prayer life, none of us can ever fully understand God and the method of asking and receiving He has set up for us. Prayer allows you to begin where you are, with the knowledge you have, however little it may be. God has made prayer so easy for us—it is simply asking Him for our needs whenever and wherever.

So Hard!

And yet, in spite of all this, it can be hard—so hard. It is hard because it requires us to slow down our lives long enough to admit that we need God. It requires us to realize that no matter how in or out of control we feel in our lives, God is the Supreme Ruler. Prayer flies in the face of self-dependence. It also requires time, determination, and focus of thought. Prayer gives no room for laziness. We do not pray because there is always something more important to us taking our time. We do not pray because we do not enjoy or feel like doing it. We do not pray because we do not really believe that God will act on our behalf. We do not pray because it goes against everything our flesh wants to do. There is such a battle—much of which takes place without our noticing it.

God cries out to us, "Pray. Ask Me. Will you realize that I want to give to you? Please depend on me. Slow down a little and think about Me. Oh, child, will you come to Me?"

All the while our flesh is distracting us from God's pleas. "Busy, busy, busy. The schedule is so crazy and I am so tired." Or, "Everything is going great and is under control.

There is no need for God. I am handling my life just fine on my own." Or, "I want to spend this day doing fun things. God is boring; it does not feel good seeking Him. I want to enjoy this time by talking on the phone, or watching TV, or reading my new book, or playing computer games, or...." But this flesh is such a liar because the reason our schedule seems out of control is that we are not asking God for help. And when we seem to be doing great on our own, our lives are truly filled with the mess of pride and selfishness. And while other activities sound so much more enjoyable, there is no full satisfaction apart from God. It is hard to do the thing that God has made so easy!

Why It Is Worth the Battle

God tells us to pray.

> *And he spake a parable unto them to this end, that men ought always to pray, and not to faint.* Luke 18:1

> *After this manner therefore pray ye...* Matthew 6:9a

> *Pray without ceasing.* I Thessalonians 5:17

> *Be careful for nothing; but in every thing by prayer and supplication with thanksgiving let your requests be made known unto God.* Philippians 4:6

Jesus Himself prayed while He lived on this earth. Abraham prayed. Moses prayed. David prayed. The disciples prayed.

Paul prayed. Verses concerning prayer are scattered throughout the Bible. It is unquestionably clear that God desires us to come to Him and pray as well.

The lack of prayer is sin.

It makes sense that, because God commands us to pray, to do otherwise is to break one of his commands. Yet how often we fail to see our prayerlessness as sin! We may admit that we do not pray like we should. We may even determine to try harder. But rarely do we confess it as sin. But it is sin—a sin, in fact, that we ought to hate.

God hears prayer.

> *The LORD is nigh unto all them that call upon him, to all that call upon him in truth. He will fulfil the desire of them that fear him: he also will hear their cry, and will save them.* Psalm 145:18-19

> *The LORD is far from the wicked: but he heareth the prayer of the righteous.* Proverbs 15:29

It is easy to fall into the routine of uttering a few words of prayer each day without ever praying to the God that hears. Mealtime prayers can be an example of this, though they do not have to be. Many people mindlessly utter the same words day after day. They are not talking to a living and hearing God. They are not really expecting God to answer their prayer. They are acting as if God is not even there. But He is there and He readily wants to hear *your* prayers. He wants *you* to come to Him with the desires of your heart. He wants *you* to turn to Him for help in time of need. He wants *you* to ask Him. There are days that "seem" like God is so far away and that He does not hear you. Sometimes it may "feel" like you are praying to the ceiling. Yet no matter how it seems or feels, never forget that God does hear the prayer of the righteous.

Prayer is the way to get what we want and need.
It sounds greedy and selfish to pray simply to get. But it is God's plan. It is not, however, some mystical, hocus-pocus, pull your desire out of a heavenly hat. It is part of a relationship between you and the living God. Also involved in that relationship are: confessing sin, seeking to know God through His Word, obeying His will, and the giving of thanks and praise to Him. What God wants in this relationship is for you to grow in dependence upon Him. As a mother, I have worked for years to make my children more independent of me, teaching them to dress themselves, feed themselves, use the bathroom on their own, and brush their own teeth. That teaching needs to continue until they are capable of living completely independently of me. God wants exactly the opposite for us. He teaches us so that we may realize that we are incapable of living any part of life independently of Him. Asking God to provide for us what we could never provide for ourselves (which is everything) is a large part of that dependent relationship. God, not man, established prayer. And He wants you to experience answered prayer.

> *Call unto me, and I will answer thee, and shew thee great and mighty things, which thou knowest not.* Jeremiah 33:3

Ask, and it shall be given you; seek, and ye shall find; knock, and it shall be opened unto you: For every one that asketh receiveth; and he that seeketh findeth; and to him that knocketh it shall be opened. Matthew 7:7-8

Do you work hard and yet struggle to understand chemistry? Ask God to help you in it. Do you need to know where to go to college? Ask God to show you. Do you need some extra money for an activity coming up? Ask God to provide. Do you have an unsaved friend or family member? Ask God to open their eyes to the truth of the Gospel. Are you lonely? Ask God for a good, godly friend. Are you overcome by a temptation? Ask God to deliver you from it. Do not live on without a dog, put up with an old vacuum, or go without God's help in your conversations simply because you did not ask for it.

Prayer is a vital part of your preparation for the future.

Trust in the LORD with all thine heart; and lean not unto thine own understanding. In all thy ways acknowledge him, and he shall direct thy paths. Proverbs 3:5-6

I do not want to miss out on God's best for my life — now or later. And I need and want His direction. How can you or I ever know what to do, where to go, or how to serve apart from heavenly direction? Thankfully, we have the promise of God's leading. But notice the prerequisite that goes along with that promise — our dependence. Trust the Lord. Do not lean or depend upon yourself; but acknowledge, seek, ask Him.

Faithful is he that calleth you, who also will do it.
I Thessalonians 5:24

Again, can you see our utter dependence on the Lord? Not only is He the one to call or lead us, but He is also the One Who will do it. We have no ability of our own to do anything right. Let's stop trying and begin asking.

Abide in me, and I in you. As the branch cannot bear fruit of itself, except it abide in the vine; no more can ye, except ye abide in me. I am the vine, ye are the branches: He that abideth in me, and I in him, the same bringeth forth much fruit: for without me ye can do nothing....If ye abide in me, and my words abide in you, ye shall ask what ye will, and it shall be done unto you. John 15:4-5, 7

The future is bright — very bright. We can go to God and ask for anything. What a shame it would be to miss out on that bright future simply because we never stop to acknowledge God in it, because we seek independence instead of abiding dependence — because we do not ask. In your life, remember to ask.

JOURNAL THOUGHTS

❑   I realize that my prayerlessness is sin, and I am making the decision to confess that to God.

❑   My thinking about prayer has been wrong in these ways:

❑   I can see that I have not been depending on God because I have not been asking for His help in these areas of my life:

❑   I see the need to begin praying about/for these things:

CHAPTER SEVEN

The Best Spot

With whom did you play hide and seek when you were a kid? Likely, it was with your brothers, sisters, or cousins at family get-togethers, with your classmates on the school playground, or with the neighborhood kids. I grew up in a very kid-friendly neighborhood, mostly because there were lots of us. It was great during summer break—there was almost always some sort of game or activity to be involved in. We did not often have an excuse for being bored. There was only one problem. It was a neighborhood filled with boys. I usually had plenty of playmates as long as I was willing to play street hockey or look for frogs in the nearby pond. But if I felt like playing dolls, I was on my own. I could not hand-pick my playmates. I could not decide to move into a girl-dominated neighborhood instead.

You probably did not pick out your playmates either. You could not hand-pick your neighbor. You had no control over where you went to school or who your classmates would be. Your childhood companions were, for the most part, handed to you.

Though you are not a child anymore, many of the circumstances of your life are still out of your control. You likely have not decided where you live. You may have had no choice concerning your schooling. You probably do not even get to decide what you are going to eat for dinner. While all of this is true, far too many young women take a passive approach to the decisions in which they *do have* the freedom to choose. They simply accept the friends that show any interest in them—that seem to accept them. In wanting friends and acceptance, a young woman will carelessly follow those friends around. If those friends go to the movies, then she goes too. They go to a party; she goes too. She continues to follow the circumstances that are handed to her, even though now she has the freedom to choose differently.

Little Freedoms, Big Results!

Julie is a nice, talented young woman. She has an attractive personality and is good looking as well. She grew up going to church and was taught the principles of the Bible. And for the most part, her goals for her future were good. I am convinced that she dreamed of a life that included serving God and marrying a godly man. She may have even envisioned herself and her future family serving on a mission field. Her goal was, as would be anyone's, to have a happy, successful life. But as a teenager, Julie did not take the best advantage of the freedoms that were given her. Instead of spending time with a girl of good character from church, she was known to be hanging out at the mall with her unsaved friends. While she did join in on youth group activities, she also joined in on her public school dances. She readily accepted the worldly friends and entertainment that seemed to fall into her lap. It was sad, but not surprising, to hear that she was not doing well. Although she is still in her early twenties, her life is in shambles. She has shattered her own dreams of a good future. This is not where she ever expected to be. When did it happen? Was it when she made a decision to go to a secular college instead of a Christian one? Was it when she began dating around in that college? Was it when she stopped going to church? Was it when she got involved in illegal activities? All of those things did send her spiraling down farther from her dreams of a successful life, but the decisions that began the shattering of those dreams happened much, much earlier. While she made some good decisions for God in her teen years, she never forsook that overall passive attitude with her choices. I do not think it ever dawned on her that the seemingly small decisions that she made every day as a young woman would greatly affect her future. But they did.

What are your goals for the future? To serve God? To marry a wonderful, loving, godly man? To one day have a picture-perfect home with father, mother, and children? To be a good wife? To use your talents in a ministry? Do not be fooled into thinking that where you go and who you spend time with today will not affect those goals. Use whatever amount of freedom given to you to choose the best possible spot now. You may have no choice about where you go to school. You may have no control over a family member's worldly influence. You may not even have the freedom to go to a good, Bible preaching church. Do not spend your time worrying about all the things you cannot control; spend your time making sure that the choices you do have the freedom to make are the best ones.

> *And he [Israel] said unto him [Joseph], Go, I pray thee, see whether it be well with thy brethren, and well with the flocks; and bring me word again....And when they saw him afar off, even before he came near unto them, they conspired against him to slay him....And Judah said unto his brethren, What profit is it if we slay our brother, and conceal his blood? Come, and let us sell him to the Ishmeelites, and let not our hand be upon him; for he is our brother and our flesh. And his brethren were content. And they took Joseph's coat, and killed a kid of the goats, and dipped the coat in the blood; And they sent the coat of many colours, and they brought it to their father; and said, This have we found: know now whether it be thy son's coat or no. And he knew it, and said, It is my son's coat; an evil beast hath devoured him; Joseph is without doubt rent in pieces.* Genesis 37:14a, 18, 26-27, 31-33

Joseph had some pretty bad circumstances about which he had no control. He was sold as a slave to a pagan group of people who had no fear of God. He was surrounded by bad influences. And to make matters worse, his master's wife tried to seduce him to sin with her. Yet as a young man, Joseph focused not on what he had no control over, but made sure that with what very little freedom he had, he chose the best and right things. It is true his future did not end up the way he might have imagined it would, but it did end with success — in fact, such great success that he became the second in command over Egypt. He not only saw his father and brothers again, but also saved their lives during a great famine. His greatest success was that he followed God's will for his life.

I feel confident that you have more freedom in your life than Joseph did. But to find yourself in a successful future, you must use those freedoms to choose the "best spot" now. Get into that position by being in the right places with the right people.

The Right Places

Where can you get help in your preparation for the future? Where are you most likely to learn how to serve God? Where are you most likely to meet a godly young man? Where are you most apt to find friends who encourage you to do right? Where are you going to have the most help staying away from temptations? Here are some opposite questions to consider. Where are you most likely to be encouraged to be worldly? Where are you most likely to meet a guy who cares only about physical relationships? Where can you find friends who care nothing about doing right? Where can you go to most please yourself and your flesh?

Every time you are faced with a decision about where to go and spend your time, you need to ask yourself these questions. Put yourself in a position to succeed.

School

You may very well have no control about where you attend junior high or high school. I did not either. But there are decisions within that school that likely are yours to make. Seniors in my school had a Senior Lounge, where they could spend their lunch hour, with couches and a TV always set to MTV. I had a choice. I could join most of the other seniors in the lounge, or I could eat my lunch in the cafeteria with the underclassmen. I also had some freedom in choosing classes and teachers. Most public schools will allow students to go home instead of attending pep rallies and dances. Proms are usually optional. You likely have the freedom to choose whether to participate in band, choir, plays, and sport teams or not. You may have to accept public school, but you do not have to accept everything that is offered you within that school.

My husband attended public school through his freshman year of high school. The summer before his sophomore year, he attended a church camp and was encouraged to seek after a Christian education. There was a good Christian school about twenty miles from his home, but it was not cheap and did not have a bus service. He was willing to accept "no" for an answer but decided to share with his parents his interest in switching to that Christian school. Though it would cost both time and money, his parents agreed to let him make the switch. And it unquestionably changed his future. By simply asking, he was granted permission to put himself in the "best spot."

You may not know if your parents would even consider such

a change. But it would have been a shame if my husband had missed that opportunity to be in the "best spot" simply because he did not ask. With a submissive attitude, ask. The answer may be "no." And if so, you can rest in it. But the answer could surprise you. Perhaps the choice is left up to you. Do not settle for public school attendance if there is a good Christian school in your area, and your parents are willing to send you there. Do not put yourself in a position where you will be taught things that oppose the Bible if homeschooling is an option. Certainly never fuss at your parents if they have chosen homeschool or Christian school for you. Do not wish for public school attendance instead. Seek to be in the "best spot" possible.

Anna was saved at the age of thirteen when a local church reached out to her. She grew in the Lord and attended that church all throughout her teen years. Unfortunately, she did not have the support of her family in her Christian life. But that did not deter her desire to please God. She had no choice but to attend public school. It was hard, but with a submissive heart she sought to do right. With any freedoms she was given, she chose the "best spots."

Erin lived in the same town and went to the same church. She had Christian parents who led her to the Lord when she was six. She was a sophomore in her Christian school when her best friend transferred out of the same school and into public school. The rest of that year Erin watched her best friend have "the time of her life" in that public school. She began to long for what she called "a taste of real life." That summer she began a campaign to convince her parents to allow her to transfer as well. She pleaded, but it soon became evident that her parents were not going to change their minds. She graduated from that Christian school but hated her last two years there. She resented never being able to experience the fun and freedom of public school.

Who do you think was found serving the Lord eight years later as a pastor's wife? It was Anna. Was it because public school gave Anna more opportunity to succeed than Erin? Certainly not. It was because while Erin, who had better circumstances fought against the good and helpful influences in her life, Anna sought for the "best spot" possible.

Church

> And let us consider one another to provoke unto love and
> to good works: Not forsaking the assembling of ourselves
> together, as the manner of some is; but exhorting one another:
> and so much the more, as ye see the day approaching.
> Hebrews 10:24-25

You need the support of a Bible-believing, Gospel-preaching church. You need to be provoked (or stirred up) unto love and good works. You need to be exhorted and encouraged by other believers to keep growing, to do right, to serve God. And you need to exhort and encourage other believers as well. You need to consistently hear the preaching of the Bible. You need the help of a pastor and his wife. You need a place where you can meet and befriend other Christian young people. You need to be around mature Christian women.

The aged women likewise, that they be in behaviour as becometh holiness, not false accusers, not given to much wine, teachers of good things; That they may teach the young women to be sober, to love their husbands, to love their children, To be discreet, chaste, keepers at home, good, obedient to their own husbands, that the word of God be not blasphemed.
Titus 2:3-5

Do not take church lightly. If your parents allow you to attend, you should be there every time the doors are opened. Sometimes you will have a conflict of interests. Do you go to church Sunday evening or go to the park with your friends? Attend church or be involved in an extra curricular activity? Church or babysitting job? Really the choice is "best spot" or less than best. If the decision is yours to make, pick the "best spot." It is no small thing and can make the difference between a successful or shambled future. Do not forsake it!

Activities

There is nothing wrong with fun. My husband, children, and I often play games, take walks, visit zoos, enjoy the company of others, shop, share jokes, take vacations, and sometimes even sit around doing nothing. We all need enjoyment, relaxation, humor, and fun in our lives and would be in rough shape without it. But those types of activities need to fit into the "best spot" as much as anything else. It is unfortunate that many young people hold on to the thinking that Christians cannot have fun. They view the dedicated Christian life as boring. But it does not have to be that way. Fun does not have to involve sin. It is ironic because the teenagers I have met that mock right living never seem happy themselves. They do not look relaxed; they rarely smile and often look downright miserable. Having fun and doing right can go hand in hand.

College

Secular universities, prep schools, and community colleges are full of wickedness. Alcohol, sexual perversion, drugs, and even witchcraft run rampant on these campuses. The classes are often taught by agnostic professors who promote godless thinking and living. Students are encouraged to "question" their authorities. They are taught to live for themselves. Christians are asked to reconsider their beliefs and open their arms to all the religions of the world.

> *Beware lest any man spoil you through philosophy and vain deceit, after the tradition of men, after the rudiments of the world, and not after Christ.* Colossians 2:8

Why put yourself in the path of those who will try to spoil you?

> *And have no fellowship with the unfruitful works of darkness, but rather reprove them.* Ephesians 5:11

Why surround yourself with the dark wickedness of the world?

> *I will set no wicked thing before mine eyes: I hate the work of them that turn aside; it shall not cleave to me.* Psalm 101:3

Why set unnecessary temptation before your eyes?

Enter not into the path of the wicked, and go not in the way of evil men. Avoid it, pass not by it, turn from it, and pass away.
Proverbs 4:14-15

If you have the freedom to choose—do not enter into the path of the wicked. Do not enter a secular college.

There are several Christian colleges in this country whose primary purpose is to encourage students to live in submission to the Bible. They will certainly prepare you in your chosen area of study, but their primary goal is to graduate students who will go on to serve the Lord.

My parents gave me the freedom to choose my college. I knew the "best spot" for me was Christian college. I sought God's direction concerning which Christian college to attend, and He led me. It was at that college I met some people who worked at the Bill Rice Ranch and encouraged me to consider spending a summer there as a counselor. The Bill Rice Ranch is where I met my husband. Where would I be now had I not chosen the "best spot" then? Will your college choice affect your future? More than you can imagine!

The Right People

Be ye not unequally yoked together with unbelievers: for what fellowship hath righteousness with unrighteousness? and what communion hath light with darkness? And what concord hath Christ with Belial? or what part hath he that believeth with an infidel? And what agreement hath the temple of God with idols? for ye are the temple of the living God. II Corinthians 6:14-16a

These verses tell us that we have no business binding ourselves together with unbelievers. It is not telling us that we should never be in the same room with them or that we should never talk to them. It gives us no excuse to be rude or unkind. But it does command us to avoid close relationships with them. Our friends should be believers. We are to separate ourselves from the world.

Be not thou envious against evil men, <u>neither desire to be with them</u>. For their heart studieth destruction, and their lips talk of mischief. Proverbs 24:1-2

My son, if sinners entice thee, consent thou not....My son, <u>walk not thou in the way with them; refrain thy foot from their path</u>. Proverbs 1:10, 15

Blessed is the man that <u>walketh not in the counsel of the ungodly, nor standeth in the way of sinners, nor sitteth in the seat of the scornful</u>. Psalm 1:1

<u>I have not sat with vain persons</u>, neither will I go in with dissemblers. I have hated the congregation of evil doers; and <u>will not sit with the wicked</u>. Psalm 26:4-5

<u>Love not the world</u>, neither the things that are in the world. If any man love the world, the love of the Father is not in him. For all that is in the world, the lust of the flesh, and the lust of

the eyes, and the pride of life, is not of the Father, but is of the world. I John 2:15-16

The failure to follow these Bible commands was one of the primary causes of Julie's shattered life. She did have some good Christian friends, but she also embraced the companionship of the unsaved—even dating them. She walked with the ungodly; she stood with sinners; she sat with the scornful. She loved the world. She was enticed to sin. By not separating herself from the ungodly, she ruined her opportunity for a wonderful, God-blessed future.

It is important—vitally important—in your preparation for the future that you place yourself in the best spot with the *best people*. Be wise in your selection of friends avoiding these common pitfalls:

Pitfall #1 — "Perfect" Witness
The Bible unquestionably commands us to share Jesus Christ with the unsaved world.

Go ye therefore, and teach all nations, baptizing them in the name of the Father, and of the Son, and of the Holy Ghost. Matthew 28:19

The book of Acts is full of stories of believers coming into contact with unbelievers for the purpose of the Gospel. Jesus ate in the homes of wicked, unsaved men so that he could share with them the truth that He is the way, the truth, and the life. We are commanded by Christ Himself to be fishers of men. You are not in complete obedience to God unless you are involved in soulwinning. However, many Christians, both young and old, allow themselves to become too close to unbelieving friends, spending much time with them, and even growing emotionally attached. They convince themselves that the close bond is not a problem but is good. "After all," they think, "my relationship with my unsaved friend will allow me the opportunity to be a good witness. I will be a good influence on them." Many Christian young women date and even marry unsaved men under the same pretense. But it is a pretense that is not biblically accurate. Yes, you are to have contact with the unsaved for the purpose of sharing the gospel; but you are not in obedience to God if you are yoked together—or have close ties with them. The two commands do not conflict! You cannot effectively accomplish the one if you do not obey the other. In fact, if you choose a close relationship with unbelievers, you will be enticed to sin and likely will fall. In doing so, you will lose any hope of being a good testimony to them for Christ.

Pitfall #2—Blind Assumption
I fell into this pitfall when I first began college. Because I previously had very little contact with other believers and because I did not know much about the Word of God, I did not know there was such a thing as a worldly Christian. This was ironic because I was one. But I had the blind assumption that every saved person would be a good friend. And I fell into a crowd of rebellious believers who were far from good friends.

But now I have written unto you not to keep company, if any man that is called a brother be a fornicator, or covetous, or an idolater, or a railer, or a drunkard, or an extortioner; <u>with such an one no not to eat</u>. I Corinthians 5:11

Now we command you, brethren, in the name of our Lord Jesus Christ, that ye withdraw yourselves from every brother that walketh disorderly, and not after the tradition which he received of us....For we hear that there are some which walk among you disorderly, working not at all, but are busybodies. And if any man obey not our word by this epistle, <u>note that man, and have no company with him</u>, that he may be ashamed. Yet count him not as an enemy, but admonish him as a brother. II Thessalonians 3:6, 11, 14-15

A saved person, on his way to heaven because he has depended on Christ for salvation, has the ability to live his life here on earth with complete disregard to God and His Word.

Be ye therefore followers of God, as dear children; And walk in love, as Christ also hath loved us, and hath given himself for us an offering and a sacrifice to God for a sweetsmelling savour. But fornication, and all uncleanness, or covetousness, let it not be once named among you, as becometh saints; Neither filthiness, nor foolish talking, nor jesting, which are not convenient: but rather giving of thanks. For this ye know, that no whoremonger, nor unclean person, nor covetous man, who is an idolater, hath any inheritance in the kingdom of Christ and of God. Let no man deceive you with vain words: for because of these things cometh the wrath of God upon the

children of disobedience. Be not ye therefore partakers with
them. For ye were sometimes darkness, but now are ye light in
the Lord: walk as children of light: (For the fruit of the Spirit
is in all goodness and righteousness and truth;) Proving what
is acceptable unto the Lord. And have no fellowship with
the unfruitful works of darkness, but rather reprove them.
Ephesians 5: 1-11

The whole point of this passage is exhorting believers in Christ to *live like* believers. Do not be involved with the darkness of the world. Before you were saved, you were darkness. But now that you have salvation, you are in the light. So act like it! And do not have anything to do with works of darkness. But there are Christians who have not heeded this exhortation. They embrace the world's darkness instead of fleeing it. We are not to consider such a believer to be our enemy, but we are to separate ourselves from him or her. Pick your friends wisely, not foolishly following after the friendship of any and every believer.

Pitfall # 3—Overlooking the Obvious
Karen attended a small church in a small town community. Her desire was to live in obedience to God. Although it was difficult and she was mocked by her classmates for it, she lived a separated life. As far as she knew, there was not another saved person in her public school. There were a couple other teenagers from a nearby town who attended her church. But their time together was limited; and, furthermore, these teens were caught up in the entertainments of the world. Karen was lonely and tired of being treated like an alien. Feeling friendless, she began to

wonder if her dedication to God was worth it. During that whole time, however, there was someone in her church that was reaching out an arm of friendship to Karen. But Karen failed to see it. In overlooking the obvious, Karen missed an opportunity to fill that void of companionship in her life. The arm of friendship was being extended by her pastor's wife. It was true there was a fifteen year age difference between the two. And, yes, the pastor's wife had a husband and children to care for. But that pastor's wife would have loved to put Karen on her list of close friends. She would have enjoyed shopping with Karen, and having her over to join in on their family game time. She longed to be the friend that she knew Karen needed.

If you are dedicated to choosing your friends wisely, it may be that the pickings are slim. But do not miss out on good, godly friendships you could have just because you set age limitations.

Do not overlook your family. It may be that your parents and brother and sister are unsaved. You may constantly have to be around wickedness because your family is living wickedly. It is true that you cannot sever your relationship with them, nor should you. You should, however, separate yourself from the acts of wickedness, when you can. Do your homework in your room and away from the TV show that the rest of the family is watching. Ask if you can spend the night with a friend instead of going to the wine tasting festival with them. But above all, honor your parents and submit to them! And look for opportunities to spend quality time with them. Talk with them when you can. Take a walk with them if they will go. Bring out a game and ask who will play with you. Help them weed the garden. Certainly pray for their salvation. No one would claim that it is easy to live a godly life as a child or teen in an ungodly home. But by the grace of God, it is possible!

If you have a home that is led by saved, godly parents, be thankful for it. And do not miss out on the benefits of it. Such a family is your best source of companionship and friendship. Society tells you that it is not "cool" to be with your family. Teenagers often refuse to be seen with their parents because they are too concerned about what their friends would think. By the way, that is a sign that their friends are not good ones. I greatly admire a family that I know well. They love being together. When the kids were young, the whole family played and laughed together. When the kids were teens, the whole family played and laughed together. Now that they are all adults, the whole family plays and laughs together. They all had friends outside their family, but there was no bond greater than the one within their family. Brothers and sisters obviously enjoyed being together. The kids showed no sign of embarrassment to be seen with their parents. They did not lack for good times and companionship. They did not miss out. They did not overlook the obvious.

Pitfall #4—Bonding Buddies

I have one best friend. I love being with my best friend. When we are together we have so much fun. We often walk together. We shop together. We take the kids on outings together. My best friend and I talk a lot even sharing our innermost feelings. We encourage each other in the Lord. We pray together. I am so glad we live close by. I do not know what I would do without him. Him? Yes, I said, *him!* My one best friend is my husband. My favorite piece of home decor is a plaque that hangs in our bedroom that says, "Happiness is being married to your best friend." And it is a wonderful thing. But...what would you think if I had said that my best friend was my neighbor Bob? Or my old college buddy John? Or a co-worker Rick? It would have rubbed you the wrong way. Why? Well, because I am married. It would be inappropriate for me to have my closest friends be men. Other people would question my fidelity, and legitimately so. It just would not be right.

Yet young women frequently foster buddy-buddy friendships with young men. They spend lots of time together talking, shooting hoops, hanging out at the mall, and playing computer games. They are shocked if someone asks, "Are you dating?" Their answer, "Nooooo, we are just good friends."

Suppose a young man of marrying age, but still single, had begun to be interested in a certain young lady. But the girl was not interested in being courted by him. She told him that she would like to be good friends. The man thought, "I am not going to do that; there is no point in it." At first you and I may be tempted to think, "What a jerk. He does not even care about her if he is not willing to be just friends. He is being selfish and only cares about getting a wife." But, you know, that's not it. He would be right! What *is* the point? Let's say he agreed and they became good friends.

They strolled in the park together, they attended a ballgame together, and they went out to eat together. They became good buddies. As time went on the Lord led the girl to the man she was to marry, and the same happened to the fellow. Now that they are both married, their friendship with each other fades away. The girl's husband is not about to let his wife be buddy-buddy with some other guy. It would cause much tension in the guy's marriage if he tried to hang on to that close friendship. His wife would not like it at all. And it would not look good. So what was the point of the buddy-buddy friendship in the first place?

Can you have appropriate, casual friendships with guys? Of course! My husband and I have many male friends. Are they buddies? To my husband, yes. But to me, no! It is not wise for a woman to foster "buddy" relationships with men. To do so is not healthy and is not the "best spot" to be in.

Pitfall # 5 — Poor-Me Pity

> *Then Jezebel sent a messenger unto Elijah, saying, So let the gods do to me, and more also, if I make not thy life as the life of one of them by to morrow about this time....And he came thither unto a cave, and lodged there; and, behold, the word of the LORD came to him, and he said unto him, What doest thou here, Elijah? And he said, I have been very jealous for the LORD God of hosts: for the children of Israel have forsaken thy covenant, thrown down thine altars, and slain thy prophets with the sword; and I, even I only, am left; and they seek my life, to take it away. I Kings 19:2, 9-10*

I can almost hear the whine in Elijah's voice as he said, "*I, even I only, am left.*"

You may have a very difficult situation, as did Elijah whose life was even threatened because of his obedience to God. It sure did not appear that Elijah had a friend in the world. And he had quite a pity party because of it. If you are not careful, you may be tempted to make a pity party out of your difficult situation. "I am the only one around that is trying to live right. I am all alone. There is no one else. No one likes me. Poor me. Poor me." Listen to God's response to Elijah's pity party.

> *Yet I have left me seven thousand in Israel, all the knees which have not bowed unto Baal, and every mouth which hath not kissed him.* I Kings 19:18

Elijah pouted because he thought he was the only one serving God, while there actually were seven thousand others!

Friend, you may be lonely in your effort to please God. But you are not alone. You may not have any good friends where you live, and you may not have the support of a good family; but you are not alone. You may not have met them, and you may not know where they live; but there are hundreds and, yes, even thousands of saved people who have not bowed their knees to the world. They too are seeking for the "best spot." No, friend, you are not alone.

Winning the Game

Playing hide and seek with young children can be humorous. They have not learned the art of finding a good hiding spot. They are likely to be easily seen poking their heads out from behind trees. They might cover their heads with blankets and assume that you will never see them because they cannot see you. But older kids understand the goal: finding the perfect hiding spot. They search for the places where no one would think of looking. And they understand that if they can accomplish finding that "best spot," then they will win the game time and time again.

Hopefully, the goal of your life is to do God's will—to follow and serve Him—to be in the exact place He wants you to be. In doing so, you will have a happy and fulfilling life, one that avoids unnecessary heartache and trauma. In order to reach that goal, you must find and stay in the "best spots." If you simply throw a blanket over your head, you are not going to win the game of hide and seek. And if you simply accept all the easiest circumstances that come your way, you likely will not find yourself in the successful future for which you had hoped. When you have the option, choose the best spot now so that you can be in the best spot later.

JOURNAL THOUGHTS

❑   I have not been using my freedoms wisely because I have made these poor decisions in the past:

❑   I am making the decision to be in the right places. My thinking and actions need to change in these ways about these places:

School:

Church:

Activities:

College:

Other:

❑   I have allowed myself to be yoked together with the wrong people. My plan of action to change that is:

❑   I have fallen into this/these pitfall(s):

❑   This is what I need to do to guard myself against those pitfalls:

CHAPTER EIGHT

The Lion and the Bear

The story of David and Goliath is remarkable. So much can be learned from David's faith in God and his obedience. His courage was great; his fear of God was evident. But in the midst of all the glamour of the story, there remains the fact that David was prepared. He was a young man, yet he was ready to do battle with a giant. When King Saul questioned David's ability to face the huge enemy, David gave this answer:

> *Thy servant kept his father's sheep, and there came a lion, and a bear, and took a lamb out of the flock: And I went out after him, and smote him, and delivered it out of his mouth: and when he arose against me, I caught him by his beard, and smote him, and slew him. Thy servant slew both the lion and the bear: and this uncircumcised Philistine shall be as one of them, seeing he hath defied the armies of the living God.*
> I Samuel 17:34b-36

David had learned the skills he needed to face the task before him. While doing the job his father had given him — keeping sheep — he gained experience needed later in his life. He became excellent at handling a sling shot. David knew the battle was God's; his confidence was in God. Yet he was ready to be used of God. He had learned; he had practiced; he was prepared. Although it is unlikely God has a battle with a giant in your future, He does want you to be practiced, learned, and ready as well.

So the question is: "Learn, practice, and be ready for what?" *Everything!* Learn all you can. During this stage of your life you have more opportunity to build talents than you ever will again. As a wife and mother, I have very limited time to spend on extras. There are things I would love to learn to do that I simply do not have the time to pursue. There are talents I would love to develop but have no one to teach me. Although you are busy, and although your resources are limited as well, you do have many great opportunities during this stage of your life. But those opportunities likely will soon be gone forever.

There is a particular talent that I had the chance to learn in my youth. In fact, my parents greatly encouraged me in it. But I did not want to do it. I was bored with the effort it would take. I was lazy about it. I did not learn it. Since then, there have been hundreds of times when that talent would have been very useful to my husband, to my children, to my church, and to my ministry. But I cannot do it and no longer have the opportunity to learn. It is such a loss simply because I was too lazy. I did not take advantage of that opportunity. Do not let your opportunities pass you in that same way. Learn all you can now.

Each year at camp we bring in summer staff to help in different areas of the ministry. Included in the staff are a number of young women, most of whom serve as counselors. It is amazing to me to see the talent in these college-age girls. I remember one year in particular when each one of them had ability in an area we needed that summer.

We had two counselors who had learned sign language. Another girl had spent much time learning medical skills. One girl knew horses; she had more riding experience than anyone else we had on staff. Another was a picky cleaner. (While that may not sound glamorous, it was an important, practical, needed skill—one that I have discovered many women do not have.) There were two with outstanding musical ability. We needed and used each one of those talents and more that summer. I cannot imagine what it would have been like if they had not learned those things. Unquestionably, our camp would have suffered. I do not know how God will use them and their talents in the future. Certainly, He will. But I do know He used them greatly—in one summer alone.

It is such a temptation to be lazy. Because we have other things we want to do, we put off and put off and put off until it is too late. It is sad but true that many young people learn only what they are forced to learn. They enter adulthood unprepared, unable to be fully used by God.

How long wilt thou sleep, O sluggard? when wilt thou arise out of thy sleep? Yet a little sleep, a little slumber, a little folding of the hands to sleep: So shall thy poverty come as one that travelleth, and thy want as an armed man.
Proverbs 6:9-11

The soul of the sluggard desireth, and hath nothing: but the soul of the diligent shall be made fat. Proverbs 13:4

Slothfulness casteth into a deep sleep; and an idle soul shall suffer hunger. Proverbs 19:15

Has your laziness cast you into a deep sleep? Have you been lulled into thinking that it does not matter? Wake up before you find yourself greatly lacking.

What You Can Learn

Cooking, piano, a foreign language, landscaping, computers, sewing, volleyball, child care, singing, care for animals, cleaning, typing, song writing, interior design, first aid, teaching, playing an instrument, money management, horsemanship, poetry, paper crafts, photography, swimming, speech, drawing, grammar, basketball, accounting, flower arranging, softball, entertaining, sign language, hair styling, quilting, gardening—and there are so many other possibilities. Obviously, no one person could learn to do all these things well. It is also true that you do not need to dedicate all your time to something you hate doing. But the point is that you *can* develop *some* talents. You can practice and become good at them. There may be areas in which you have been given natural ability. Develop them. There may be areas in which you have no natural ability and no possibility of gaining that ability. Do not sit around feeling sorry for yourself; go out and find some things that you can learn to do. Do not allow your focus to become so set in one area that you learn nothing else. I have met great basketball players that could do nothing else well but play basketball. I have met piano players who could do nothing else well but play the piano. These young women soon find that there is more skill needed in life than playing basketball or the piano. Take advantage of all the possibilities. You will be glad you did.

How You Can Learn

Take opportunities.
Many opportunities will fall into your lap. That was true with David. He was told to watch sheep. In doing so, he saw the need sheep have for a shepherd and used the comparison to write one of the most comforting Psalms — Psalm 23. During that time on the mountainside, he played the harp to entertain himself. All the practice made him so accomplished that he was summoned to play for the king. In his dedication to protect the sheep from lions and bears, he became a man of valor, later claiming victory in many battles. But all would have been much different if he had murmured about his job. "Why do I have to watch the stupid sheep? That lion can have the lamb — one less for me to have to deal with. This is so boring; I never get to do anything I

want to do." He would not have been prepared to write the Psalms, play music in the palace, face the giant, lead armies into battle, or be king himself had he not done his best in the job handed to him. It set the course for the rest of his life. Do not buck against the circumstances for learning that God has given you now. Do you have chores to do on the farm? Do your best. Who knows how God may use the skills you gain. Are you told to watch your little brother? Clean the bathroom? Write a paper? Help in the family business? Whether you are in public school, Christian school, home school, or college—opportunities are there. Your classes themselves are important. Do your best in math, history, grammar, accounting, Spanish, chemistry. God does not throw dice to determine your circumstances. He is bringing those things to you to make you ready. Do not spoil the plan.

Make opportunities.

If your situation allows, take an extra class to learn computers, sign language or speech. Get involved in a sports team or music group. Perhaps your parents would be willing to provide you with some private lessons in art or horsemanship. Many do not have that opportunity but can learn from friends, relatives, neighbors or church members. All around you are people with talents. Many of those people would be thrilled to take some time to teach you. Grandparents can be a wonderful source of help. And never underestimate what you can learn from your parents. I am so thankful for the skills my parents taught me, many of which I now use on an everyday basis. Ask your father to teach you to change a tire. Ask your Mom if you can do some of the cooking. Show interest in their talents; ask them to teach you. Certainly never fuss at them when they are taking the time to instruct you or giving you an opportunity to learn. Become involved in your church. Perhaps you can join the choir and learn to read music. Maybe there is a Sunday school teacher who would love to have you as an assistant. Do you have a friend who is good at crafts? Ask her to teach you some things. Do you have an aunt with a small child? Ask her if you can spend some time learning baby handling skills from her. Look around and you will find all sorts of people with all sorts of abilities. Take advantage of it.

Begin Using Them Now

Use your talents, abilities, and time now. You do not need to wait until you are twenty or thirty to serve God. As you are learning, serve. Have you learned to cook? Offer to make a meal for your family once a week. Are you good with kids? Volunteer your services to someone in your church who cannot afford to hire a babysitter. Have you learned to be a picky cleaner? Help clean the church or your home. Are you good in math? Offer to tutor a fourth grader who struggles. Not only will you be a help to others, you will become more proficient in that ability.

At the same time, do not force your help on someone who does not want it. Your parents, pastor, or teacher may think it is best for you not to help in a certain area. Be willing to accept "no" for an answer. But do not let that hurt or scare you away from asking how else you can be a help. It is always sad when a person keeps her talents in a box. As a quiet person, I am tempted to sit back and watch the world around me. I watch others in their great musical ability. I envy those with bubbly personalities. I see all the beautiful crafts a friend makes. I marvel at how quick-minded a co-worker is. And then I do nothing but feel sorry for myself. In that pride, I refuse to use the abilities I have. How selfish!

I am told of a lady who served in a variety of ways. Because of her husband's leadership position and her outgoing personality, she became well-known. With the popularity, she began to change. She was no longer willing to do behind-the-scenes jobs. She would not clean a bathroom, help make a meal or watch the nursery. Although she could not see it, she stopped serving others and began serving herself. Again, how selfish! The reason to expand your talents is to use them—all of them.

They Belong To God

David knew that he and his talents belonged to God. When faced with the enemy, he did not depend on his skill. He trusted in God. He fully believed that he would have victory because he knew God was in it. Notice to whom David gave credit for the defeat of the lion and the bear.

> *David said moreover, The LORD that delivered me out of the paw of the lion, and out of the paw of the bear, he will deliver me out of the hand of this Philistine. And Saul said unto David, Go, and the LORD be with thee. I Samuel 17:37*

When victory came to David time and time again, he boasted in his God. He gave God the glory for what was done. He did not glory in himself.

> *So likewise ye, when ye shall have done all those things which are commanded you, say, We are unprofitable servants: we have done that which was our duty to do.* Luke 17:10

Do not pride yourself in your talents. Even in your greatest success, you are only an unprofitable servant. You have only practiced and worked hard because God enabled you to do so. Your ability belongs to God. Do not draw attention to yourself. Never look down upon or snub another person because you think you are more capable. On the other side of things, it is easy to snub a person who is talented *because* of her talent. It is not fair for you to judge her and assume she is snobby simply because she has ability. You may very well be guilty of more pride than she. When a person realizes that she and her talents and sometimes lack thereof belong to God, pride vanishes away. David gloried in His God. Make God your glory as well.

JOURNAL THOUGHTS

❑ I need to expand my talents. I want to learn to:

❑   I realize I need to do my best with these opportunities that already exist:

❑   I have these ideas to make more opportunities:

❑   I am going to seek to serve now by:

❑   I am making the decision to confess to God these specific proud thoughts/actions:

CHAPTER NINE
Hidden

"Sire, I announce the arrival of a messenger from the land of Zenobia. He brings you a gift from King Orithel."

"A gift from Orithel? Bring him in."

Moments later the messenger appeared before the throne of King Desiderius. "Oh, great King Desiderius," began the messenger, "my lord King Orithel has sent me with kind greetings of prosperity to you and your kingdom. A gift of rare beauty he desires to share with you if Your Highness will accept."

"I readily accept any gift from Orithel," the king replied. The messenger placed a square chest as long as a man's forearm before the king, bowed before him and took his leave. "A gift of rare beauty indeed," the king quietly whispered, "and of great value, no doubt."

The chest would have taken the highest skilled craftsman years to complete. It was a masterpiece—the fine detail perfect on every side and outlined in pure gold. So priceless was the gift, King Desiderius knew he must at once send a messenger to King Orithel with words of thanks. But to put into words appreciation for such a gift was not an easy task.

After days of deliberating, King Desiderius sent the messenger. The trip would take four days by horseback. Days were long for Desiderius as he waited to hear if King Orithel would accept his words of appreciation. To offend the king of Zenobia could mean an end to the twenty-two years of peace between the two lands. Eight days later King Desiderius was informed that the messenger, who was now on foot, would arrive in minutes. In urgency, the messenger had run his horse so hard that the horse had collapsed the day before in exhaustion. The mind of King Desiderius raced. What could a message so urgent mean? Had he offended King Orithel? Was he facing war? Finally the messenger arrived barely able to speak.

"Sire, the message from King Orithel is that the gift...Oh, King Desiderius...the gift from King Orithel is inside the chest."

King Desiderius dismissed everyone, wanting to be completely alone when he opened the chest. He could not keep his hands steady while lifting the lid. Under a pure white silken napkin was the largest and purest ruby known to man. He had been so impressed by the beauty of the chest itself that it never dawned on him to open it. Inside lay hidden the rarest and most valuable treasure of all.

> *...man looketh on the outward appearance, but the LORD looketh on the heart.* I Samuel 16:7b

There is no question but that God is interested in the heart of man. It is not uncommon to hear people talking about it. "Inner beauty is the most important beauty." If I were to be honest, however, I do not think I would take it as a compliment to hear someone say of me, "She sure is a beautiful person on the inside," because often such a compliment is code for: "Boy, is she ugly, bless her heart." Emphasizing inner beauty seems only a small consolation when it appears young men only notice those with perfect features and figures. You cannot go to a mall or see a commercial without realizing that looks are important. It sometimes seems that's all people notice. So what good is inner beauty to someone average looking? The truth is that it is of great value; in fact, it is priceless. It is also extremely rare — even among Christian women.

Surprised? If you are, it is probably because you have a misunderstanding about what this true hidden inner beauty is. It is not personality. I have been with fun, enjoyable personalities who show no sign of this hidden beauty. I know very kind, compassionate women who lack this most valuable beauty. There exist very intelligent, talented, and capable women who do not have even a trace of it. Others will stand in awe of one who holds this beauty, though they may not understand why. They may not be able to specifically identify the hidden beauty in her, but they will know there is something dramatically different about her. They may even be irritated by her because they can tell she has something that they are lacking. A man with a wife who holds this hidden beauty will likely be admired by other men because of her. She is a rare treasure indeed.

This rare, hidden beauty is not inherited, but obtained. And it is obtainable by any woman who wants it. Do you want it? You can have it. You can be a rare, priceless gem. It is completely possible but not easy. It rubs against the grain. It is like trying to walk in a crowd of people going the opposite direction of everyone else. It is challenging to say the least. And when your own flesh wants to betray you and send you sprinting in the opposite direction, the challenge is heightened. But it is worth it to be a woman with this rare, hidden beauty that will be noticed by God and man. In fact, it is God who has described it.

Likewise, ye wives, be in subjection to your own husbands; that, if any obey not the word, they also may without the word be won by the conversation of the wives; While they behold your chaste conversation coupled with fear. Whose adorning let it not be that outward adorning of plaiting the hair, and of wearing of gold, or of putting on of apparel; But <u>let it be the hidden man of the heart</u>, in that which is not corruptible, even <u>the ornament of a meek and quiet spirit, which is in the sight of God of great price.</u> For after this manner in the old time the holy women also, who trusted in God, adorned themselves, being in subjection unto their own husbands: Even as Sara obeyed Abraham, calling him lord: whose daughters ye are,

as long as ye do well, and are not afraid with any amazement.
I Peter 3:1-6

A woman with true inner beauty is one who adorns herself with a meek and quiet spirit. She is a submissive wife. Disappointed? I can understand. It certainly does not seem glamorous. In fact, it definitely rubs us the wrong way. And it is hard to believe that it has more value than a pretty face. However, God is no liar, and He has clearly stated that the hidden man of the heart that is adorned with submission is far more valuable than the costliest beauty enhancer.

But I Am Not Married!

While God does not work in odds and percentages, you likely will marry someday. Regardless of whether there is a wedding in your future or not, you should be preparing yourself to be a wife. And there is no greater attribute of a wife than submission. Furthermore, the mark of a God-honoring woman, married or not, is submission to God and those in authority over her.

Favour is deceitful, and beauty is vain: but a woman that feareth the LORD, she shall be praised. Proverbs 31:30

Let every soul be subject unto the higher powers. For there is no power but of God: the powers that be are ordained of God. Whosoever therefore resisteth the power, resisteth the ordinance of God. Romans 13:1-2a

You can obtain that rare hidden beauty even before marriage. And by living that submissive life now, you will also be preparing yourself to be a submissive wife. No one is born with submission. It does not come naturally. I am a fairly socially quiet person—that is my natural personality. I struggle chit-chatting with others, especially people I do not know well. I feel obviously awkward. My lack of social ability, however, is not an indication of a submissive heart. Although it could be surprising to anyone who does not know me well, I am also very much a "take the bull by the horns" person. My husband could readily verify this! While much good can come from my "let's get it done" personality, it often wants to prod me out of my bounds and into rebellion. Submission is *not easy* for me. Often outgoing women can be found excusing their rebellion by saying, "That's just the way I am." It is as if they think that submission is easier for the socially quiet ones. While the outcropping of rebellion may vary, the truth is that rebellion comes easily to all. That is the way we all naturally are. Submission is not coincidental or a natural part of personality.

Magic Wedding Ring

Sam and Sandra were in love—really, really in love. They were convinced they wanted to spend the rest of their lives together, and so they began to proceed with marriage plans. Naturally, they wanted the wedding to take place as soon as possible. There was only one problem: Sandra's parents. They were determined that Sandra should finish her bachelor's degree first. Graduation was two long years away. Sam was already a college graduate and had promise of a good job. Sandra pleaded and even stooped to whining. Sam asked his parents to try to convince her parents it would be a good thing for them to marry earlier. But Sandra's parents were unmovable—college graduation first. And since her parents were the ones who would be footing the bill for the wedding, Sam and Sandra felt stuck. They finally resolved that they would have to wait. But they were not happy about it. In fact, it seemed all their time together, which was little since Sandra was away to school most of the year, was spent griping about Sandra's parents.

"Why don't they understand how hard it is on us to wait? Why do I need a degree anyway? You have a good paying job. Maybe they just want to make me miserable. It sure seems that way. They are being so unreasonable."

Graduation day finally arrived and the wedding day a week after that. It was a beautiful wedding. Sandra had found the perfect dress the previous fall. The flowers and cake were exactly as she had envisioned, and Sandra's best friend from college, Janet, flew in to be her maid of honor. Having been a voice major, Janet provided outstanding music. Sam watched as Sandra came down the aisle. He had been waiting for her for so long. And now she was to become his wife. They turned toward each other to say their vows. Sam was first. Then it was Sandra's turn.

To have and to hold, from this day forward,
For better, for worse,
For richer, for poorer,

In sickness and in health,
To love, cherish, and obey,
Till death do us part.

Sam then took the ring, placed it at the tip of Sandra's finger, and said, "With this ring I thee wed." As he pushed it back into place on her finger, a mystical electric current came from the ring and pulsed through Sandra's body. Though harmless, it was magical. For from that point on, Sandra became a submissive woman obeying and honoring Sam, now her husband. And they lived happily ever after—Sam loving and providing for Sandra, and Sandra reverencing Sam.

You have figured out that this is not a true story. Yet if Christian young women think about submission at all, they make it out to be some sort of fairy tale. They are convinced that although they fuss and buck against their parents and other authorities in their lives, they will be perfect, sweet little wives. Let's make the story of Sam and Sandra more realistic.

Sandra thought it would be easy to submit to Sam. It was different than her relationship with her parents. She and her parents could not see eye to eye, but she and Sam agreed about everything. There had been a couple arguments while they were engaged, but they always worked it out. It did not take long, however, for Sandra to realize that Sam was not the flawless decision maker she thought he would be. Only two years after marriage, Sandra found that Sam was spending more and more time at work. She did not understand why. But Sam did. He was tired of hearing Sandra's fussing and complaining, and he dreaded coming home to it. It seemed she never stood in support behind him. She always had a better idea and even accused him of being unreasonable. He once overheard Sandra tell her mother how stingy he was being for not replacing the carpet. He wanted to give her what she wanted but was afraid it would send them into unrecoverable debt. She just could not understand his reservations. Their marriage certainly was not picture perfect.

It all sounds a little familiar. Remember Sandra's attitude toward her parents? She could not understand why they were being so unreasonable. Now she could not understand why her husband was so difficult to live with. Sam was not perfect; he did make some mistakes. And Sandra could see only *his* failures. She was blinded to the fact that her lack of submission was slowly tearing her marriage apart just as she had been blind to her own rebellion against her parents as a girl. In her eyes, she was wiser and a better decision maker. If she did not step in, she thought, her husband would surely lead them down a road to unhappiness and disaster. Yet it was strange. Whenever Sam gave in to her and she got her way, she found it never brought her the happiness she thought it would. She thought marriage would rescue her from the unhappy teen years at home. But now she found herself as unhappy as ever.

There is no magic wedding ring that makes a submissive wife out of a rebellious young woman. The best thing you can do *now* to prepare yourself to be a submissive wife *later* is to obtain that hidden beauty *now*. Submit yourself to the authorities God has given you *now*. It is not a matter of personality or circumstances. It is a matter of the will. It is a decision. Do you want the rare hidden beauty of the heart? Are you willing to be submissive?

Why? Why? Why?

Two-year-olds are famous for their questions. "Here, Jamie, take the purple popsicle." "Why?" "Emily, Look at the cute little doggie!" "Why?" When the child reaches the age of four or five, their "whys" change and make a little more sense. "Dad, why is the sky blue?" "Grandma, why did the cat have four kittens?" Soon the "whys" change again. "Mom, why do I have to go to bed at eight? All my friends get to stay up till nine." "Why can't I ride my bike to the store?" It seems there is something within each person, even at a very young age that makes us feel like we must know the why behind everything.

As a mother, I have learned the right response to the "why" question. It is, "Because I told you so." My children have learned it is not worth their time to question me about why I have set a rule or asked them to do something. It is the same answer each time. Whether I could explain to my children the reasoning behind what I have told them to do is beside the point—for them. The number one thing they need to understand is that "because Mom said so" is a good enough answer to "why?" They will eventually understand the reasoning behind many of our family rules. And often

I will explain the reasoning to them because they need to be taught, but not as a response to a rebellious "why." I am their mother, and they are my children. It is their primary job to obey whether they understand or not.

Why has God commanded children to obey their parents? Why does God command wives to submit to their husbands? Why God? I can almost hear His stern voice as He replies, "Because I said so."

> *Wives, submit yourselves unto your own husbands, as unto the Lord. For the husband is the head of the wife, even as Christ is the head of the church: and he is the saviour of the body....Nevertheless let every one of you in particular so love his wife even as himself; and the wife see that she reverence her husband.* Ephesians 5:22-23, 33

> *Children, obey your parents in the Lord: for this is right. Honour thy father and mother; which is the first commandment with promise.* Ephesians 6:1-2

> *Wives, submit yourselves unto your own husbands, as it is fit in the Lord....Children, obey your parents in all things: for this is well pleasing unto the Lord.* Colossians 3:18, 20

We need not understand it any better than that. Remember "you no makka the game, you no makka the rules"? Are we so proud in our thinking that we will not obey God unless His way makes sense to us? It will never make sense without a heart that is willing to obey. Why should you obey your parents now? Yes, it is true it will help prepare you to be a good wife later. And, yes, it will instill within you a rare, hidden beauty. And, yes, it does make sense. But the one primary reason is because God said so. Why should I as a wife honor and obey my husband? Yes, it will help make me a good wife. And it will instill within me that rare, hidden beauty that I so desire. And, yes, it even makes sense. But the answer to my "why" question gets no better than an "I told you to" by God.

Traps

I hope you have been stirred to make a decision for submission. If so, you need to be able to recognize some traps you will find along the way. I've seen several types of animal traps: mouse traps, rat traps, bug traps, fox traps, bear traps, and even skunk traps. They all look different, but all have the same goal — to capture the animal. The traps waiting for you along your path of submission do not all look the same. Some do not hide what they are as well as others. Some are hidden beneath harmless looking covers. The results of the traps vary in intensity, but their goal is all the same — to capture you. They are rebellion traps. They are laid out waiting for me as a wife. They are also laid out waiting for you as an unmarried young woman. They want to catch us both, married or not. But also, they know that catching you now before you are married will make it easier for them to catch you again later when you are married. Learn to watch out for them and strive to avoid them at all costs.

Trap #1 — Refusal

This one is pretty obvious, but it is a trap nonetheless. If you disobey authority, you have fallen knowingly into a rebellion trap. It does not matter if you get away with it. It does not matter if it is small and seemingly insignificant. Disobedience is always disobedience.

Trap #2 — Heart Murmur

I do not recall the details surrounding it, but I remember a time when I fell into this trap as a wife. It was in the morning, and my husband had made a decision I did not like. After he left for work, I hopped in the shower with a very bitter heart. Although no one was around to hear, I remember muttering complaints to myself about him. He never knew anything about it, but I had quite a heart murmur. I obeyed him outwardly in the sense that I would have done what he told me to do, but my attitude was anything but honoring. A heart murmur is a destructive rebellion trap — whether others know about it or not. Do not be deceived into thinking you are fulfilling God's command to obey authority if you have such a heart murmur against them. There is no beauty in that.

Trap #3 — Griping

The Bill Rice Ranch has coined a definition for griping — *Saying anything to anyone in a derogatory manner when the person to whom you are speaking can do nothing about it.* You would be guilty of griping if you complain to your friend about a rule your parents have set. Guilty as well would be a group of students gathered together in the hallway who fuss about the unfairness of a teacher. A wife would be guilty of griping when she gets involved in what I call "husband bashing." When enjoying the company of other women, she says, "I wish my husband would do something about the leaky faucet. I have asked him and asked him. But he just lets it drip on and on. You would think he would consider the water bill, but he is just too lazy to do anything about it. I told him if it is not fixed by the end of the weekend, I was going to call a plumber. I guess all men are alike. You can never get them to do anything around the house."

Griping is a subtle trap because it is so readily accepted in our society. Everyone does it. But it is wicked rebellion.

Trap #4—Arguing
"But...Mom...." Often the familiar question "why" comes out in this trap. "Why can't I go to the party?" You do not really care why; you are simply arguing! To argue with your parents or any authority is rebellion. A wife who argues with her husband is not being submissive. She is trying to sway him to her way, her opinion, and her wish. There is no obedience in that. There is no honor in that. A wife is to be obedient both when she agrees and when she disagrees. Without argument.

Trap #5—Cold Shoulder
This is usually an outcropping of a heart murmur. When we are displeased and perhaps even angry at the actions or decisions of our authority, we tend to disregard the warm relationship that is supposed to exist and replace it with a cold, unresponsive one. It is our way to express our unhappiness and even get back at our parents or husband.

And it usually works too. Your parents and my husband are concerned and even hurt by our coldness to them. The cold shoulder ends only when either we finally forget about it or when the authority makes an effort to "patch things up." If they come to us, we achieve some sense of victory in the situation.

In a grocery store men's restroom, my husband read a sign that said, "The dog called. He wants his house back. Visit the floral department." It is a clever advertisement; but, unfortunately, the idea of a husband being in the doghouse is a much too common one. Only a rebellious wife would put her husband there. But what society expects is for the man to buy flowers or some other gift and try to patch things up—even if he was simply taking the leadership role in the marriage. The wife is seemingly victorious in her rebellion. Let that never be said of your future marriage. And let that never be said about your relationship with authority now. Do not give your parents the cold shoulder. What may feel like a victory for you is truly a great loss.

Trap #6—Sabotage

My husband will be the first one to admit that he has a poor memory. It is often tempting for me to use that poor memory to my advantage. For example, if he makes a decision concerning our family finances that I do not think is the best, I am tempted to think, "I will just wait a couple weeks and bring it up again with my suggestion. He will not even remember what he said he wanted to do with that money anyway." If I fall into that temptation, I have fallen into the sabotage trap.

The sabotage trap is when you intentionally give a matter less than your best effort because you do not think it is a good idea or decision. I once knew someone who in his work was a very negative person. It was not uncommon to hear him say, "That will never work." And if it were left up to him, the idea would fail. Not because it could not succeed, but because he did not want it to and did not give it his best effort. It was amazing how in similar situations that were to his advantage, it would work out; it happened. I do not think he realized it, but he was living his career life in the sabotage trap. In the end, he sabotaged himself yet could not understand why there was failure.

When you are asked to do something by your parents, husband, or any authority — give it your all even if it does not profit you in any way. To do otherwise is not obedience.

Trap #7—Assumption

The summer cowboy wanted to take a female camp co-worker on a private horse ride, but my husband, the camp director, was in town to lunch. When driving back on the camp, my husband spotted the two horse riders. The cowboy rode up to him and said, "I was going to ask you, but you were not here. I didn't think you would mind." Whether the horse ride was acceptable or not was irrelevant. That cowboy assumed permission. He had fallen into the assumption trap.

My children have grown to the place where they do not need to ask about everything because they *know* that the answer would be a definite "yes" or definite "no." But if there is a time in which they are not sure, they had better not assume permission. They have learned what to do when we are not available to ask and they are forced to make a decision. They think, "What would Mom and Dad want me to do?" It is not uncommon for them to come home saying something like, "I didn't go to the playground with my friend because I didn't think you would want me to." It also would not be uncommon for me to say, "It would have been all right for you to go, but I am glad you didn't because you didn't think I would want you to. But next time it would be fine for you to go."

When my husband was young, he often heard his mother say, "If in doubt, leave it out." That is a lot different than assuming permission. As a wife, I do not seek my husband's permission for everything I do. But I live my life in light of it, asking when I am not sure.

Trap #8 — Disregard

"If you know the answer will be 'no' don't ask — just do it. After all, it is easier to get forgiveness than permission" is the voice of the Disregard Trap. It may be easier, but it is not right. In fact, it is simply a disguise for Trap #1 — Refusal.

Trap #9 — Doormat Syndrome

What about your rights? We live in a liberal society so caught up in personal rights. The women's liberation movement exists to make sure women are not slighted in what they would call a male-ruled world. They want women to have equality — the right to decide, to do, and to be like men. They are appalled at the thought of the old-fashioned wife — one who stayed at home cooking, cleaning, and taking care of children while her husband went out and worked to support the family. It would make their blood boil to hear someone tell them that they should be submissive to their husbands. After all, they are equal with men and have their rights. They are not about to be the doormat for some man.

It is true that, as a woman in America, you have rights. There is no government official that is going to force you to live in light of the biblical position on marriage with the husband as the head of the home. You have the American right to rebel against your future husband. You can demand a 50%-50% marriage. You can join in on the philosophy of the women's liberation movement. But do not be fooled into thinking you are obeying God while you do it.

The amazing truth is that true freedom comes when we choose to follow God's way.

> *Proverbs 31:10-12 says, "Who can find a virtuous woman? For her price is far above rubies. The heart of her husband doth safely trust in her, so that he shall have no need of spoil. She will do him good and not evil all the days of her life."*
> *This good woman, this obedient woman, has earned the complete trust of her husband. Since she is committed to doing what he wants her to do, there is no conflict of interest. He knows she won't betray him before business associates or friends. Her every act, her every thought, does him good.*
>
> *Verse 23 says her husband is "known in the gates" and that he "sitteth among the elders of the land." Her husband has risen*

to great honor; he is a leader in the city. That is listed as a fruit of the virtuous woman. Why? Because a virtuous woman supports her husband, encourages him, makes it possible for him to be a leader of men. Verse 28 says her children will call her blessed and her husband will praise her.

Is this obedient woman a wimp, a doormat, a mindless robot doing only whatever it is her husband capriciously decides? Oh, I hope you will not get that impression! (Me? Obey Him? Elizabeth Rice Handford, pp. 69-70)

Trap #10 — Correction

My family and I were visiting a family full of girls. Throughout a meal, the wife and girls subtly undermined the father's authority, correcting him when he did not get a story just right. "Actually Dad, it was Fred's son, not his daughter who did that." "Oh, that did not happen two years ago," the wife would interrupt. "It was actually three years ago." The whole time, the wife and daughters would giggle at this man's "stupidity." And all the while, these women were the ones who looked foolish.

Men are often accused of maintaining an "I'm right" attitude. Yet women tend to be just as guilty, putting in the last "right" word. Our views and opinions are the right ones, and we feel a burden to make sure everyone around us is convinced of our position. If they cannot be convinced, we make sure they at least know where we stand. I had a friend that loved to debate with her parents, her husband, church members, and friends. She was very quick-minded and could voice her arguments faster than her hearers could process all the

information. She would often verbally win these debates —
even if her opinions were dead wrong. She rarely listened to
another person's view always proclaiming, "The way I see
it is...." She was right; she had the best ideas; she knew the
correct way of doing things. In all that, she was quick to find
fault with other people, including those in authority over
her. Since her husband could not keep up with her verbal
debates, he could not maintain the leadership role in the
family. He followed where she lead him. All the while she
assumed she was a submissive wife because she *would* obey
him if he asked something of her. She fell into the subtle
Correction Rebellion Trap.

Beware if you find yourself to be a bossy person. Beware
if you are frequently correcting others. Beware if you are
always promoting your opinion and idea (even if they are
right ones). Beware if you tend to recognize only faults
in authority figures. Beware if when you are asked to do
something you reply, "Oh, I was just about to...." It is not
easy to recognize the Correction Trap, but it is a deadly one.
Watch for it and flee as soon as you see any sign of it.

Trap #11 — Guise of Righteousness

My husband had preached to a group of ladies about
the importance of submission. After the service, a visibly
bothered woman approached him, shook her finger in his
face and explained to him that if she did what he preached,
her unsaved husband would make her do things that were
unquestionably wrong. Yet her facial expressions and
body language portrayed her rebellion. Actually this lady
was not so much concerned about being forced to sin by

her submission to her husband as she was disgusted at the idea of being submissive at all. Her rebellion was written all over her face. She had fallen into the Guise of Righteousness Trap.

I have counseled a young woman who disagreed with her parents about a biblical issue. She was distraught. She was tender. She just wanted to do the right thing. There was no rebellion in her questions. She had a sweet, submissive attitude. She simply did not know what to do in her situation and was asking for guidance. There was no Guise of Righteousness there.

Both women in these stories had legitimate difficult issues. But there was a great difference. The one approached her submission problem with a submissive heart and in a submissive way. The other was in complete rebellion. Do not ever use your need to be righteous as an excuse to feed your rebellion.

Trap #12 — Manipulation

Kids of divorced parents often use this trap to their advantage. Jane lives with Mom who will not give Jane permission to attend the next weekend's party. But Jane isn't worried, because she spends the weekends with Dad. He will give permission. Yes, it may cause yet another phone fight between Mom and Dad. But after all, that is nothing new. If Jane is going to have to live in a divorced parent home she might as well make the best of it.

The manipulation trap in marriage is a little harder to

describe, but I do not believe there is a wife who does not acknowledge it exists. It seems every wife has the great ability to manipulate her husband. She gets him to do what she wants or to make a favorable decision. All the while, he thinks he has come up with the idea himself. He thinks the decision was his. He has been manipulated and does not even know it.

When I asked my husband to help me think through the different rebellion traps, I mentioned the Manipulation Trap. He actually came up with the divorced parent illustration, but he could not comprehend it within marriage. He is a very intelligent man, yet he has been manipulated by me more times than I would care to admit. And he was surprised to hear about it. He had no idea. Wives are good at manipulation. Getting away with it, however, does not make it right. Shame on me and shame on any woman, young or old, that has fallen into this trap. Rebellion it is.

Make It as Easy as Possible

There are no *ifs, and*s, or *but*s about it. Submission to authority can be hard — very hard. There is no personality or magic wedding ring to make it easier. Our very sin nature is appalled at the thought of it. While there is nothing you can do to make it easy, there is something you as an unmarried young woman can do to make it as easy as possible. Marry carefully!

It is amazing how many women suffer through difficult

marriages because they chose to marry an ungodly, disobedient, and selfish man. They are stuck. They have to follow him even though he has little or no character. They have to live with a man that is harsh and cold toward the things of God. He has no burden to lead the family in a good and right direction. He provides no guidance for the children. He makes unwise decisions that cause the whole family to suffer. He does not love. He is not trustworthy. He is not faithful. Submission to this husband, but for the grace of God, is unbearable.

I enjoy, however, observing the marriages of many of our closest friends. Submission for the wives is difficult, but not because their husbands make it so. It is difficult because submission is difficult. These, my friends, have chosen to marry into the best possible situation. They have husbands who are imperfect and do make some unwise decisions. But they are husbands whose hearts are set toward pleasing God. They desire to do right—to follow and serve the Lord. They desire to lead and keep their families in the middle of God's will. They train their children to fear God. Their love for their wives is obvious to all around. As married couples, they have fun. They smile, laugh, and are relaxed. You can even observe them holding hands—after having been married for years! They have not lost the sparkle in their eyes for their mate.

In this day and time, you likely are able to choose your mate. You can reject or accept a marriage proposal. Why make the difficult task of submission more difficult than it needs to be by marrying someone insensitive to the things of God?

There exists no perfect man. But there do exist men who love the Lord and strive after righteousness. Wait for this type of man. Pray God will send you such a man. Accept no less. It is better not to marry at all, than to marry into misery.

When I was college aged, my mother began praying for my future mate. She was not concerned so much about his looks or talents. She could have prayed I would marry someone financially set. She could have asked for someone who would want to live close by. But as far as I know, she only asked God for one thing concerning my finding a mate. She prayed that God would lead me to a man after God's own heart. I am thankful for her prayers. I am thankful for God's answer. My primary job as a wife is to be submissive. It is not an easy task. I often fail. But I am blessed to be in a marriage where it is made as easy as possible. Determine now to accept nothing less for yourself in your future marriage relationship.

*NOTE: For additional help concerning a wife's submission, please read *Me? Obey Him?* by Elizabeth Rice Handford. For more information concerning purchasing a copy, contact the Bill Rice Ranch.

JOURNAL THOUGHTS

❑   I want to have the rare, hidden beauty of submission.

❑   I can see that I have not been submissive to my present authorities in these ways:

❑   I have fallen into these rebellion traps:

❑   I need to take these steps now to avoid those traps in the future:

❑   I realize that submission is hard even in the best possible situation. I am making the decision that if God leads me to marry in the future, I will only consider a man if he is living in obedience to God.

DATE: _____

CHAPTER TEN
Out of Bounds

Eight-year-old Scott was to move across the country in just three weeks. He was excited about the potential adventures that awaited him in Maine, but he was also sad to leave his friends. Even though things were hectic with packing, he persuaded his parents to let him have one last weekend sleep-over with his closest friends. Two of his school buddies, Chad and Gregory, came as did his neighbor, Michael, who lived a mile down the road.

The boys slept late on Saturday morning because they had stayed up past midnight the night before playing computer games. They grabbed a quick breakfast and were just about to head out the door when Mrs. Foster stopped them by saying, "Now boys, have fun out there, but I don't want you to cross any fence lines today—our property only. Okay?"

Chad quickly piped up, "But Mrs. Foster, we were really hoping to be able to explore in the woods today."

"I'm sorry," she replied, "but I just can't let you play there today. We have six acres here; you still have plenty of room to explore."

The disappointed boys went outside and sat around poking sticks into the ground as they tried to decide what to do next. They finally came up with a game of their own making that was similar to hide and seek and involved water balloons (which is not the smartest thing to do on a crisp October morning, but boys will be boys).

Since it was his house, Scott was "it" first. With a water balloon in each hand and two more in each pocket, Scott headed off in search of his friends. It was not long before he found Michael and Gregory. After a few more minutes of looking, Gregory commented that Chad must have found a really good hiding spot.

"Come on, guys," Scott pleaded. "Help me find him. I am soaked and getting cold. I want to go ask Mom if she will make us some hot choc...."

"Look over there!" Michael exclaimed pointing off into the woods. The boy's eyes followed Michael's finger and soon spotted a large man dressed in bright orange coming out of the woods.

"It's a hunter," Scott said, "and it looks like he's carrying a deer. He must have gotten one already."

"Let's go ask him if we can take a look at it," Gregory

responded. The three boys spirited towards the woods but stopped suddenly as they realized that the man was not carrying a deer. He was carrying Chad.

The hunter called out to them, "Hurry, go call 911! A boy's been shot."

Chad was rushed to the hospital where he had to undergo surgery to remove the bullet from his leg and repair damage. All went well at first; but after a couple of days, infection set in. Ultimately, Chad's leg had to be amputated.

It is a sad story. So much heartache and pain was caused by Chad's disobedience! His life and future were altered forever, all because he chose to play out of bounds. It is just as sad that many young women have their futures altered as well, all because they choose to play around with things that are out of bounds for them—biblically out of bounds.

But fornication, and all uncleanness, or covetousness, let it not be once named among you, as becometh saints.
Ephesians 5:3

Dearly beloved, I beseech you as strangers and pilgrims, abstain from fleshly lusts, which war against the soul.
I Peter 2:11

The idea of being clean or keeping your purity is probably not a new one to you. Most people, however, think of their purity in context of only one specific area. But it is truly much broader, involving several different areas of your life.

It is vitally important for you and for your future that you keep away from *all* out-of-bounds areas.

Mind Boundaries

People are always commenting to my husband and me about our children's imagination. They do have vivid imaginations and frequently use them. In fact, it seems they can do nothing without turning it into some sort of fictitious play. When my son is helping my husband do chores around the house, he says, "Dad, let's pretend...." They do not just ride their bikes, they barrel race on their wheeled horses. We do not merely take hikes as a family; we become adventurers in the wild searching for something that is missing, always on the watch for wild animals. Chairs become trains; sticks become guns and whips; and large rocks become tables and chairs at a restaurant. It is not uncommon at meal time to have to remind them that they need to eat their food, not create things out of it.

While they are so creative in their play, they are also very predictable. If we visit a museum, we can count on the fact that they will set up their own museum the next day. After we visit a zoo, they play zoo. In the summer when we are heavily involved in summer camp, they play it all. They pretend to have cookouts; they become lifeguards; they do skits; they have services leading music and preaching; they hold pretend Bill Rice Ranch rodeos. The reason that their imaginative play is so predictable is that it has to be fed.

What do you think would happen if, instead of being protected from the evils of the world, my children were heavily exposed to them? What would they play if my husband and I were involved in alcohol and drugs? What would they play if we frequently watched pornography and had a fast and loose lifestyle? We know what the sad answer would be. Why do they not play such things now? The reason is because there has not existed anything to feed that kind of imagination.

While you have outgrown playing make-believe, you do still have an imagination. That imagination and those thoughts, which will result in your words and actions, are very much affected by what you feed your mind. There is no delete button on your brain. While it is true we forget many things, the image of something filthy is not likely to be one of them. You need to put a purity boundary around your mind by not allowing anything wicked to come into it via your senses (primarily eyes and ears).

I will set no wicked thing before mine eyes: I hate the work of them that turn aside; it shall not cleave to me. Psalm 101:3

Had David kept his eyes from wickedness at all times, he would not have committed adultery with Bathsheba.

And it came to pass, after the year was expired, at the time when kings go forth to battle, that David sent Joab, and his servants with him, and all Israel; and they destroyed the children of Ammon, and besieged Rabbah. But David tarried still at Jerusalem. And it came to pass in an eveningtide, that

David arose from off his bed, and walked upon the roof of the king's house: and from the roof he saw a woman washing herself; and the woman was very beautiful to look upon.
II Samuel 11:1-2

David was supposed to be in battle. He chose to be in the wrong place at the wrong time. The result: he saw something he should not have seen. That feeding of his mind sent him somersaulting down a road of great sin and tragedy.

Though Eve's sin did not involve immorality, the feeding of her eyes and ears played a big role in her fall.

And the serpent said unto the woman, Ye shall not surely die: For God doth know that in the day ye eat thereof, then your eyes shall be opened, and ye shall be as gods, knowing good and evil. And when the woman saw that the tree was good for food, and that it was pleasant to the eyes, and a tree to be desired to make one wise, she took of the fruit thereof, and did eat, and gave also unto her husband with her; and he did eat.
Genesis 3:4-6

Eve *listened* to the serpent and went so close to the forbidden tree that she could *see* how appealing it was.

Keep thy heart with all diligence; for out of it are the issues of life. Proverbs 4:23

In other words, put a boundary around your heart or mind. The following verses explain how to keep that fence up.

Put away from thee a froward mouth, and perverse lips put far from thee. Let thine eyes look right on, and let thine eyelids look straight before thee. Ponder the path of thy feet, and let all thy ways be established. Turn not to the right hand nor to the left: remove thy foot from evil. Proverbs 4:24-27

Keep your eyes straight ahead on the path of righteousness. Do not allow them to turn and look upon anything impure. Pay attention to where you go, not allowing yourself to enter any place that could cause you to stumble.

Verse 23 implores us to put a boundary around our mind. It is not going to just happen. You must keep at it—keep at the task of guarding your heart. By the way, the need for mind boundaries does not end at marriage—it must continue throughout all stages of life. A married woman who allows wickedness to enter into her mind is as guilty as an unmarried person who has done the same.

The world and the devil want to snare both married and unmarried alike into disregarding the need for mind boundaries. They have been very successful as well, using a number of different tactics. Our society, even Christian society, has become numb to the impurities around it to the point of welcoming these impurities. They watch impure things, read about them, and have close companionship with them. Most do not even realize how saturated their minds have become with the filthiness of the world. And likely it is available to *you* on a daily basis!

Beware of television and movies!

There can be little found on the screen that does not promote impurity and immorality. Soap operas are full of it. PG movies allude to it. Many game shows make a joke of it. Sitcoms drip with it (even the oldies). Half-time shows and commercials during sports games are terrible. The news, while reporting actual occurrences, can relay stories that none of us need to hear. Talk shows feel no embarrassment and often promote ungodly lifestyles. And even cartoons can portray it. Yes, even cartoons! A couple of years ago my children and I were watching a video of an old cartoon—so old that it had been remade to add color. In the last segment, two roosters fought over a hen. But this hen was no ordinary hen; she walked, talked, and held herself like a harlot. It was made to be very sensual. And this cartoon hen would easily teach its young viewers how to do the same. Young girls do not need to learn how to be like that. Neither do teenage girls, married women, or old ladies. Is your purity important to you? Then keep your heart and mind away from things that promote the opposite.

Beware of books and magazines!

A picture-less book has the ability to rob your mind of as much purity as Hollywood does. Fiction and nonfiction writers alike can be very descriptive, informing you of things that you never need to know or think about. Romance novels are dangerous. Certainly stay away from all secular ones, and even be very wary of Christian ones. There exist Christian writers who do not see any danger in unmarried couples kissing and touching. They romance the readers into wanting those things—the things that are to be reserved for a marriage relationship. They can promote the idea of dating around and becoming emotionally attached in boyfriend/ girlfriend relationships. I have personally found that even "clean" Christian romances have an unhealthy effect upon my marriage. The reason is that many of those books portray a very average female main character. I can feel what she feels, I can understand what she is going through; I can become her. But the male main character is different. He is usually the knight-in-shining-armor type. You do not read of faults; he is perfect. He is therefore unrealistic. Reading about him can cause me to feel unsatisfied with my good and God-given husband. At the very least, we ought to proceed only with caution.

Magazines can also promote immorality. That is obviously true with pornography. It is not only men who battle with that sin. Avoid ever seeing it for a first time. Teen magazines and even homemaker magazines can be filled with sensual adds and "how to" articles. Stay away from all advice columns whether in magazines or newspapers since the focus of many of the questions is immorality.

Everywhere, we are encouraged to read. While reading can often be a good replacement for television, not all reading is good for you. Be selective; your purity of mind is dependent upon it.

Beware of music!

The message of almost all non-Christian music is love. While that sounds sweet, it is not. The love that it promotes is "out of bounds" love. Soft rock, hard rock or rap—they all want you to feel the want of love; they want you to feel the need to be fulfilled; they want you to feel sensual. Country music drips with the same only from a different angle.

But it is not just the message; it is also the beat. The beat does nothing more than promote fleshly desires that are sensual and impure. It is for that reason that while the words may be fine, Christian rock is wrong and dangerous. It takes the sound and beat from the world and puts Christian words to it. But it still has the same effect: instilling an overwhelming desire to feel. There is no purity of mind in that!

Beware of companions!
A good friend is not one who will compromise your purity of mind. Your friends are not the people from which you should learn about the "facts of life." Your friends are not friends at all if they make light of and joke about things that are off color. And certainly you should never hang around people that encourage you to "loosen up." You are treading in dangerous waters if you do not eliminate close contact with such people.

> *Finally, brethren, whatsoever things are true, whatsoever things are honest, whatsoever things are just, whatsoever things are pure, whatsoever things are lovely, whatsoever things are of good report; if there be any virtue, and if there be any praise, think on these things.* Philippians 4:8

How can we think only on these good things if we feed our minds with the opposite?

Modesty Boundaries

One of the definitions of the English word *modest* is "bashful; not bold; shy; held back by a sense of what is fit and proper." It also can mean "not calling attention to one's body; decent." And yet another definition is "not thinking too highly of oneself; not vain; humble" (*Thorndike-Barnhart Comprehensive Desk Dictionary*, 1951). There seems to be great variety in these definitions, yet all three play an integral role if a person is to live a truly modest and pure life.

That they may keep thee from the strange woman, from the stranger which flattereth with her words. For at the window of my house I looked through my casement, And beheld among the simple ones, I discerned among the youths, a young man void of understanding, Passing through the street near her corner; and he went the way to her house, In the twilight, in the evening, in the black and dark night: And, behold, there met him a woman with the attire of an harlot, and subtil of heart. (She is loud and stubborn; her feet abide not in her house: Now is she without, now in the streets, and lieth in wait at every corner.) So she caught him, and kissed him, and with an impudent face said unto him, I have peace offerings with me; this day have I payed my vows. Therefore came I forth to meet thee, diligently to seek thy face, and I have found thee. I have decked my bed with coverings of tapestry, with carved works, with fine linen of Egypt. I have perfumed my bed with myrrh, aloes, and cinnamon. Come, let us take our fill of love until the morning: let us solace ourselves with loves. For the goodman is not at home, he is gone a long journey: He hath taken a bag of money with him, and will come home at the day appointed.

With her much fair speech she caused him to yield, with the flattering of her lips she forced him. Proverbs 7:5-21

A harlot, a woman who uses the sin of fornication for financial profit, is about as drastic of an example of immodesty as exists. Notice that she is the opposite of every definition of modesty. She is loud and stubborn, not held back by a sense of what is proper. She has the attire of a harlot, clothing that definitely sets her apart; it draws attention. And her speech obviously shows that she is proud and vain as she brags about all the wonderful things she could offer him. While none of us would probably identify ourselves with her, we can learn much about modesty and the lack of it from her. I hope you will make it a personal goal to flee from any even slight similarity between you and this woman in Proverbs 7.

The harlot is forward!

The immodest harlot does not blush easily and shows no sign of being bashful or reserved.

She is loud and stubborn; her feet abide not in her house. Proverbs 7:11

An immodest woman is not held back by being ladylike or proper. She does not think twice about being inappropriately bold. The purpose of her loud and stubborn voice is to draw attention to herself. It is not uncommon today for a woman to walk right up to a man that she does not know and introduce herself making it plain that she is interested. She likely laughs loudly sending a message to all around that she is a fun woman. She may even engage herself in inappropriate conversations. She is not the stay-at-home type; she wants to go out and see the world. You will often find this type of woman seeking out a place where she can be the center of male attention.

For by means of a whorish woman a man is brought to a piece of bread: and the adulteress will hunt for the precious life. Proverbs 6:26

Therefore came I forth to meet thee, diligently to seek thy face, and I have found thee. Proverbs 7:15

An immodest woman also engages in manhunts. She chases men; she pursues relationships. It seems as if that is her only goal in life. She is not happy if she is not with a man. I have had the opportunity to observe several young women, who, though far from being harlots, have wholeheartedly given themselves to being forward. They so desire to be in a relationship that they set being proper and ladylike aside. They write letters, make phone calls, and often "just happen" to bump into a particular young man. They are frequently found hanging out with the guys. Their eyes are always searching for the available males in the crowd. I have heard of old unmarried women playing the chasing game as well. They send cards and make meals for the widowers in their church. And their motive is not to be kind and helpful; it has only one purpose—to get that man. Forwardness is never modest.

The harlot is flirtatious!

To deliver thee from the strange woman, even from the stranger which flattereth with her words. Proverbs 2:16

For the lips of a strange woman drop as an honeycomb, and her mouth is smoother than oil. Proverbs 5:3

That they may keep thee from the strange woman, from the stranger which flattereth with her words. Proverbs 7:5

A harlot knows that flattery is a powerful tool, because all men enjoy being admired. The *American Heritage Dictionary's* definition of the word *flatter* can help us to see that practicing flattery is truly immodest.

Flatter: To compliment excessively and often insincerely, esp. in order to win favor (The American Heritage Dictionary, Second College Edition, 1982)

Why did the harlot in Proverbs flatter? To get what she wanted; it was entirely selfish! Anytime you compliment other people as a means to gain favor and what you want, you are guilty of flattery. Does it fit within the definitions of modesty when a woman uses flattery to woo the attention of a man? It certainly is not a humble act! And there is no sense of bashfulness or being proper involved. Do not mimic the practices of the Proverbs harlot; keep your lips from flattery.

The harlot is flaunting!
1. In her body language

Lust not after her beauty in thine heart; neither let her take thee with her eyelids. Proverbs 6:25

Body language is significant. The harlot uses even her eyelids to tempt the passerby. Several years ago, I observed a two-year-old girl flirting with an adult man. While the adults were visiting in his living room, the child leaned her arms back on a coffee table pushing her body forward. She then cocked her head to one side, looked at this gentleman, smiled at him and batted her eyelashes. The flaunting was obvious to everyone in the room. What can appear humorously innocent at age two, however, would be far from funny if it continued throughout the girl's life. She needed some lessons concerning modest body language. Flaunting body language is equivalent to advertising. That is exactly what the harlot was doing—advertising herself. If you do not want to advertise the same message that she does, you need to make sure that your body language does not resemble hers. Do not allow your body to move or lean in any way that would draw improper attention. Do not pucker out your lips as so often seen in the models of fashion magazines. Nor should your eyes be allowed to have their mischievous stare. Be careful about cocking your head, frequently flipping your hair, or running your fingers along your neckline. It would be impossible to describe all inappropriate body language, so here is a good general rule. Do not do anything that makes you feel sensually attractive. If it makes you feel that way, then it is undoubtedly immodest.

2. In her dress

And, behold, there met him a woman with the attire of an harlot, and subtil of heart. Proverbs 7:10

I do not know what the attire of a harlot in Bible times would have been like. The details of her dress, I do not think, are as significant as the fact that her dress made her known. Again, it advertised. It drew attention. It sent a message. It flaunted. It was improper, not bashful — immodest. What would be the outfit of a harlot today? Hopefully, you have never seen one, but you could make a fairly educated guess. Her clothing would not cover enough of her body; it would be too tight and probably sheer. It draws attention to her body. Now give the description for the modern style of dress. What is the average woman of America wearing today? Her clothing does not cover enough of her body; it is too tight and probably sheer. It draws attention to her body. How about Christian women? What are they wearing to church? Likely, it does not cover enough of their bodies; the clothing is too tight and maybe even sheer. It draws attention to the body. These things should not be so. The harlot has no concern about her own purity. She knows that her dress is immodest — impure. If we are concerned about our purity, why then should we try to dress like her?

Before Adam and Eve sinned, nakedness was not a problem. There was no such thing as impurity then, not even within a stray thought. But when they ate the forbidden fruit, the first thing they noticed was that they were naked. That nakedness became a problem, such a problem, in fact, that they made themselves clothes and hid themselves. Later God provided them with animal skins to cover them. If clothing was such a demanding need immediately after the fall of man, it stands to reason that it is important for us to be properly clothed some thousands of years later as well. Do not let society be your judge concerning appropriate clothing. After all, a bikini is an acceptable way to cover nakedness to the world. I do not believe that God's covering for Adam and Eve was nearly so skimpy. God covered their nakedness — all of it.

In like manner also, that women adorn themselves in modest apparel, with shamefacedness and sobriety; not with broided hair, or gold, or pearls, or costly array. I Timothy 2:9

In this verse the word *shamefacedness* means modesty or reverence. It has the idea of downcast eyes or bashfulness. A woman who clothes herself with shamefacedness will steer far away from improper apparel. She would not wear anything exposing or anything that draws unnecessary attention to her body. She would never wear a low, revealing neckline. Nor would she put on short skirts, shorts, or bathing suits that leave much flesh exposed. Her clothing would not be the tight fitting style that emphasizes the curves that only her husband should have liberty to see. Her slits would not rise high up her leg. She would understand that there is no point to an article of clothing that is translucent. She would be cautious when bending over, making sure that her shirt did not balloon out. Although it is difficult to find modest clothing in the stores, she would be convinced that it was worth the extra effort. She would accept and obey the truth that modesty boundaries are a necessary and important part of her purity.

I realize that many of the young ladies and women who wear immodest clothing are not doing so in an effort to be like a harlot. They wear what they wear because their friends and all those around are wearing those things; they simply want to fit in. Fashion dictates their wardrobe. While some of the constantly changing fashions are perfectly acceptable, many are not. When fashion and modesty cannot coincide, choose to stay within the modesty boundaries.

The harlot is forgetful!

> To deliver thee from the strange woman, even from the stranger which flattereth with her words; Which forsaketh the guide of her youth, and forgetteth the covenant of her God.
> Proverbs 2:16-17

The harlot forsakes the good instruction that she was given as a child. She forgets God's commandments. She rebels against that which could have led to a successful God-honoring future and exchanges it for that which is cheap and unsatisfying. She does what pleases her flesh. There is nothing to envy about her life. There is nothing attractive about her. But do you follow her example? Do you forsake the good instruction that you are given by your parents or church? Do you forget God's commandments in your life? Are you rebelling against that which is God-honoring? If so, you, like the harlot, are compromising your purity.

Marriage Boundaries

Marriage is honourable in all, and the bed undefiled: but whoremongers and adulterers God will judge.
Hebrews 13:4

Marriage is a boundary. Inside marriage there are things that are honorable — they are pure. Outside marriage those same things are dishonorable or impure. It is God's command here and many other places in the Bible that the things meant for marriage stay within the bounds of marriage. He calls people who step outside the marriage boundary whoremongers and adulterers. Let that sink in. Any person who participates in activities reserved for marriage with any person other than her spouse is a whoremonger. To avoid such condemnation, we must know from God's Word what things are out of bounds.

Fornication

Flee fornication. Every sin that a man doeth is without the body; but he that committeth fornication sinneth against his own body. I Corinthians 6:18

Fornication is sin committed between people not married to each other. It includes adultery (unfaithfulness within the marriage), incest, prostitution, homosexuality, and certainly the physical union of any unmarried couple. A fornicator is not a pure person. Your virginity as an unmarried young lady is priceless.

Now the birth of Jesus Christ was on this wise: When as his mother Mary was espoused to Joseph, before they came together, she was found with child of the Holy Ghost. Then Joseph her husband, being a just man, and not willing to make her a publick example, was minded to put her away privily. But while he thought on these things, behold, the angel of the Lord appeared unto him in a dream, saying, Joseph, thou son of David, fear not to take unto thee Mary thy wife: for that which is conceived in her is of the Holy Ghost. And she shall bring forth a son, and thou shalt call his name JESUS: for he shall save his people from their sins. Matthew 1:18-21

Mary, a virgin, was espoused to Joseph. In other words, she was promised to become his wife. She was also pregnant. Before God made it known to Joseph that she was carrying a child of the Holy Ghost, Joseph was planning to put her away. Her loss of virginity, as he thought it to be, was a deal breaker. He did not want to be married to a woman who had played it fast and loose. A woman's purity is valuable—both to her and her future husband.

My husband owns a beautiful ring that he keeps in his nightstand drawer; it is a woman's ring. In fact, it used to be mine. I wore it from the time I was fifteen until the day I got married. On our wedding day, I gave my husband the ring. I have not worn it since. That ring, in my life, signified my virginity. I wore it to remind myself that I was saving myself for my future husband. The ring, and more importantly what it stood for, was the most precious gift I have ever given or will ever be able to give to my husband. It has meant a great deal to him. Giving him the ring was not difficult, especially because he gave me a new one, and I have worn it since the day we were married. While my wedding ring does not represent my virginity, it does represent a great deal. It is there all the time to remind me that I belong to him and him alone.

Ring or no ring, do not throw away such a precious gift that could one day be given as the perfect wedding gift to your husband.

Loving touches

Kissing, hugging, holding hands, caressing, and other such loving touches between a woman and any man that is not her husband is out of bounds. (Obviously, there are appropriate loving touches that can take place between a girl and her father, brother, grandpa, and uncle.) Loving touches are honorable within marriage; they are special privileges for couples who have vowed to live their lives together, not for friends of the opposite gender, not for boyfriends and girlfriends, and not for engaged couples. Our society would say, "Chill out! Relax a little. What is a little hand holding or kissing going to hurt?"

Whether therefore ye eat, or drink, or whatsoever ye do, do all to the glory of God. I Corinthians 10:31

Do these loving touches bring glory to God? Within the confines of marriage they are good and honorable (Hebrews 13:4). But outside of marriage, loving touches often lead to adultery. And furthermore, they are characteristic of the harlot.

So she caught him, and kissed him, and with an impudent face said unto him, I have peace offerings with me; this day have I payed my vows. Therefore came I forth to meet thee, diligently to seek thy face, and I have found thee. I have decked my bed with coverings of tapestry, with carved works, with fine linen of Egypt. I have perfumed my bed with myrrh, aloes, and cinnamon. Come, let us take our fill of love until the morning: let us solace ourselves with loves. Proverbs 7:13-18

This woman's "love" was not genuine biblical love. True love never produces sin. It is far more than a feeling; it is a decision to do what is right. When you love God, you will obey his commandments.

If ye love me, keep my commandments....He that hath my commandments, and keepeth them, he it is that loveth me: and he that loveth me shall be loved of my Father, and I will love him, and will manifest myself to him....He that loveth me not keepeth not my sayings. John 14:15, 21, 24a

When you love other people (including a young man), you will choose to do right by them in light of God's commands.

Owe no man any thing, but to love one another: for he that loveth another hath fulfilled the law. For this, Thou shalt not commit adultery, Thou shalt not kill, Thou shalt not steal, Thou shalt not bear false witness, Thou shalt not covet; and if there be any other commandment, it is briefly comprehended in this saying, namely, Thou shalt love thy neighbour as thyself. Love worketh no ill to his neighbour: therefore love is the fulfilling of the law. Romans 13:8-10

That is why Jesus told a lawyer that to love God and to love other people are the most important commandments, surpassing even the Ten Commandments. Because if a person truly loves God and her neighbors, she will also be fulfilling all other requirements for righteous living.

Master, which is the great commandment in the law? Jesus said unto him, Thou shalt love the Lord thy God with all thy heart, and with all thy soul, and with all thy mind. This is the first and great commandment. And the second is like unto it, Thou shalt love thy neighbour as thyself. On these two commandments hang all the law and the prophets. Matthew 22:36-40

So the harlot's touches were not truly loving. They were not pure but were self-serving and wicked. And they certainly did not bring glory to God.

In the book of I Timothy, Paul gives Timothy a number of instructions including what his relationship with people ought to be like.

Rebuke not an elder, but intreat him as a father; and the younger men as brethren; The elder women as mothers; the younger as sisters, with all purity. I Timothy 5:1-2

Timothy was to show the same genuine, tender love to others as he would to those in his own family. He was to treat them with respect. While a man would certainly be right in hugging his mother or sister, he would not do so with any sort of romantic feeling. Is it possible to hug or hold hands with someone outside of your family without that romantic feeling? Yes, but not probable.

But also notice what Paul tells Timothy specifically concerning women—**with all purity.** As a preacher, would it be pure conduct for Timothy to go around hugging and holding hands with the women in the church? No, certainly not!

Let's say that you came to visit me for a few days. You tagged along on my weekly or sometimes daily trips to the grocery store. While in the produce section, we run into my neighbor. I am so glad to see him that I rush up to him, throw my hands around his neck, and plant on him a big kiss. Would you be shocked? Would you be offended? I hope so. My husband sure would be! Why? It is not acceptable, pure behavior. If it is not proper for me as a married woman to lovingly touch a man that is not my husband, it is not proper for you as an unmarried woman either.

Flee also youthful lusts: but follow righteousness, faith, charity, peace, with them that call on the Lord out of a pure heart. II Timothy 2:22

Being a wife can be a wonderful thing. Being a single woman can be a wonderful thing too. Both can be honorable and good. Both need to stay away from out-of-bounds areas.

Ultimate Protection

I am amazed to read and hear about specialized education classes in elementary school. Eight, nine, and ten-year-olds are being indoctrinated with the "facts of life." Why? It is claimed that they need to know so that they will be protected from the dangers out there such as transmitted diseases and unwanted pregnancies. These educators would argue that kids cannot avoid the problems if they do not understand all the details about how it works. I disagree! A ten-year-old boy or girl can be well-protected from such dangers without any such knowledge—none. For that matter, a teenager can be protected from these dangers without understanding all the details. It is possible because it is not an education that protects—it is obedience.

For that reason, my goal in this chapter has not been to make sure that you understand the differences between men and women and how it all works, or even what the specific, terrible consequences of impurity are. While there may be some value to knowing it, it is not essential to your purity. Obedience is *the* essential. Many people have all the knowledge about the facts of life in the world but compromise their own purity on a daily basis. My goal *has* been to educate you, but not about "the birds and the bees." It has been to show you what the Bible commands are—to give you the biblical boundaries. But even then, it will not be the knowledge of or understanding of those commands that can and will protect. It is obedience to them. Take your purity seriously! Stay within every purity boundary.

JOURNAL THOUGHTS

❑   I am confessing to God that I have allowed my mind to be fed with impure thoughts. (Be specific in your confession to God.)

❑   These are things that I need to eliminate in my life as I seek to keep my mind pure:

❑   I am confessing to God that I have allowed my life to have similarities to the life of the harlot in these specific modesty areas:

❑   In order to live modestly, I need to make these changes:

❑   Today, I am making a decision to stay within the marriage boundaries.   **DATE:**_____

❑   These are things that I need to do in helping myself stay away from temptations concerning marriage boundaries:

Too Late (a note to those who have already sinned)

It could be that this chapter has been a very hard one for you if you have already fallen in purity areas of your life. Maybe you are now plagued with questions like, "What about me? Is there any hope now?" Friend, there is always hope in Jesus Christ. You can have his forgiveness today.

If we confess our sins, he is faithful and just to forgive us our sins, and to cleanse us from all unrighteousness. I John 1:9

Confess your sin to him now and know that He will forgive. He will not hold you guilty of that sin of impurity any longer. He promised. Claim that promise!

Now determine to keep yourself from further impurity sins. Ask God for help daily as it may be even harder for you to flee from temptation now that you have tasted the fulfilling of your flesh in that area. Get help from your parents or church leaders. And take practical steps to avoid those temptations. Sever ties with the young men in your life who are asking you to compromise your purity. Stay far from them. Also cut off friendships with other companions who may have low moral standards in their own life; they will not encourage you to stay away from sin. Flee from godless entertainments that will only feed your lusts. Expose yourself frequently to influences that will help you in the battle. For example, make sure you are reading the Bible every day. Memorize verses about purity and the sin of impurity. Attend a church where you will receive help from the preaching. Make good, godly friends who will encourage you to do right. Flee that which is evil and grab hold of that which is righteous.

I think too often young women who have lost their virginity or have been involved in improper touching throw in the towel. "After all," they think, "I have already blown it." It is true you can never retrieve your virginity once you have lost it. And it is true that the scars of improper touching will live with you for the rest of your life. But if you have confessed your sin, God sees you as a clean vessel. There is no reason to mar it again simply because you marred it once before. Live the rest of your life in purity.

CHAPTER ELEVEN

Camouflaged

The summer staff of the Bill Rice Ranch enjoys the opportunity for a little rest and relaxation on Saturdays in between camp weeks. On many of those Saturdays, activities are scheduled purely for the enjoyment of those who have given their summers to serve at the Ranch. In any given summer the bus could be loaded to head toward a bowling alley, a mall, a miniature golf course, a roller skating rink, or a state park. But often the most popular activities among the high school and college-aged young people are the ones that take place on the Ranch property. One such event has been the Tick Game; it is played after dark and involves several teams. I do not know what the main objective of the game is, but I do know that it is important for each team to avoid the "ticks" who are 10-15 Bill Rice Ranch staff men. Each "tick" finds a clever hiding spot somewhere within the several acre game radius. He wants to go undetected so that when a team comes near his position, he can suddenly jump out at them. And each time they play it, it is obvious that the ticks enjoy the game as much as, if not more than, the young people playing. These men go all out, painting their faces black and dressing in army pants. They camouflage their appearance to hide the truth about themselves so that they will not be distinguishable.

Hunters often camouflage themselves in order to blend in with their surroundings and remain undetected by the deer. Men in war use camouflage to keep from being targeted by the enemy. Criminals will camouflage themselves and sneak around in the darkness so that they and their evil deeds will not be seen. Believers in Christ, too, often use camouflaging tactics — no, not with black face paint or green and brown blotted khakis — but for the same ultimate reason as used by the criminals, army men, hunters, and game "ticks" — to hide the truth about themselves.

Some Christians do so knowingly; they purposely and deliberately conceal those truths. Others may not be as premeditated in their camouflage, but end up using the tactics because it is convenient to do so or because they just want to blend in with the crowd. Some people simply convince themselves that appearance does not matter. "After all," they think and say, "God looks on the heart." It is true that God does not need to see our physical appearance in order to know who we are and what we are like. He does have the ability to see past the outward appearance and is never fooled in His judgments of people. Look at what He told Samuel, who assumed that Eliab was to be the next king.

But the LORD said unto Samuel, Look not on his countenance, or on the height of his stature; because I have refused him: for the LORD seeth not as man seeth; for man looketh on the outward appearance, but the LORD looketh on the heart.
I Samuel 16:7

After several more of Jesse's sons passed before him, Samuel said to Jesse:

Are here all thy children? And he said, There remaineth yet the youngest, and, behold, he keepeth the sheep. And Samuel said unto Jesse, Send and fetch him: for we will not sit down till he come hither. I Samuel 16:11b

How do you imagine David to be in this story? Often we think of him as looking like a little dweeb of a kid in comparison to his good-looking, strong brothers. And we say to ourselves, "See! The handsome ones were rejected and the dirty, sloppy shepherd boy was chosen by God. Appearance does not matter." It is true that had Samuel been left to himself to pick the right king, he probably would have made the wrong choice. That is because as a man, Samuel did not have the ability to see the heart. *Man looketh on the outward appearance* was not a statement of condemnation but a statement of truth; it is a fact! Often that is all the information we have available to us as we make judgments about other people. Are we sometimes wrong in those judgments? Yes! But do not let that fact deceive you into thinking that appearance is unimportant. Look at the description of the one God did choose—David.

And he sent, and brought him in. Now he was ruddy, and
withal of a beautiful countenance, and goodly to look to. And
the LORD said, Arise, anoint him: for this is he.
  I Samuel 16:12

David was no shabby looking young man. His looks, just
like those of his brothers, were impressive. Did God choose
a sloppy, careless kid to be the next king? No, He picked one
who looked good on the outside and the inside. David had
a good, submissive heart. David loved God. And David did
not try to hide that truth from other people by camouflaging
his appearance.

Is it fair that we judge people based on their appearance?
Notice I did not ask if we are always accurate in our
judgments, but are we fair? Even those who would quickly
pipe up and proclaim, "No, it is not fair that you judge me
based on how I look!" judge other people every day by looks
alone. How do you differentiate between a policeman, a
nurse, a Marine, a Wal-mart worker and any other person
walking down the street or grocery store aisle? You judge
them by their appearance—by what they are wearing. When
you see a dirty, shabbily dressed man with unkempt hair
and an overgrown beard lying on a city park bench, what
would you call him? Homeless? A transient? A bum? Why?
If you saw someone wearing a Red Sox tee-shirt and ball
cap, wouldn't you assume that he was a Red Sox fan? What
would you think if you saw a woman with fluorescent pink
spiked hair wearing a tight leather mini-skirt and fish net
hose walking down the street? Would you make a judgment
about her? If you saw a man dressed in a Wrangler shirt and

jeans, boots, a huge belt buckle, and a cowboy hat, wouldn't you brand that fellow as a cowboy and even assume that he rides horses? Like it or not, people will make assumptions about you purely based on your appearance as well. That reason alone should cause us to take our appearance seriously and make sure that we are doing all we can to outwardly portray what is true inwardly. We as Christian women need to refuse three deceptive camouflaging tactics that will hide specific truths that should never be hidden.

Camouflage Tactic #1 — Carelessness

A careless, sloppy attitude about your outward appearance will camouflage the truth that you serve an orderly God who is concerned about details. Is there any area of life in which God is or was careless and sloppy? In the creation of the world? In His plan for salvation? In His dealings with mankind? In His will for your life? In His preparation of heaven? No! God has meticulously designed it all. But the world does not like to think of God as being precise and particular. They prefer to picture him as a laid-back, go-with-the-flow, let-everyone-do-as-they-please sort of god. When a child of God is careless in her appearance, she supports and encourages the world's wrong view of God. Does not a princess make a reflection upon the king's reputation? As it is natural for a child to bear resemblance to her parents, so we ought to make sure that our appearance brings honor to our heavenly Father.

*In like manner also, that women adorn themselves in modest
apparel, with shamefacedness and sobriety.* I Timothy 2:9a

The Bible word *modest* is different than the English word
modest that we use today which was defined in the previous
chapter. Here the word means *orderly.* Just as it is important
to maintain modesty in the English sense of the word by
wearing clothes that are proper and not revealing, so is it
important to maintain modesty as the word is used in the
Bible by making sure our dress is orderly, neat, clean and
appropriate. Are there times when it is appropriate to not
be as neat and clean as other times? Sure! I have a painting
outfit that I bring out of my closet only when it is time to
paint a room. The reason: they are clothes that I have worn
for painting in the past that have a variety of colored specks
covering them. They certainly are not the neatest clothes
that I have. I wear them when I am painting; it is fine and
appropriate at those times. But you can be sure that I avoid
being seen wearing them! I have other clothes that I wear
when I am scrubbing bathrooms or working outside in the
dirt. They are appropriate for those jobs, but I would change
before making a trip to the grocery store.

While my average, what-I-wear-everyday clothes are neat,
clean, and orderly, they also are casual. I would not wear
them to a nice restaurant, to a wedding, or to church. Why?
Because they would not be appropriate for those occasions.
The world today is pushing people to accept jeans and a tee-
shirt as suitable clothing for any and every situation. "I am
the way I am; and I am coming to church, but I am coming
on my terms wearing what makes me feel comfortable,"

are the words of one who is not willing to submit to the authority of the church. Can you hear the rebellion in that statement? That person does not want anyone—even and especially God telling her what to do concerning her appearance or any other area of her life. Do not let that be true of you. It is important to dress nicely for church. For one, it will cause you to take church more seriously than if you show up in your everyday attire. It will also be a testimony to others, both within the congregation and without, that church is important to you. I could not count the times when someone has made a comment to my family about our nice appearance on Sundays. "You all are dressed up today. Is there a special occasion? Are you getting your picture taken?" we are frequently asked. "No, we have been to church," is our reply. At the very least they will know that church attendance is important to us.

Casual is the "in" style. And there is no one who likes to be comfortable more than I do. And while there is nothing wrong with casual or comfortable, we need to beware of the sloppiness that tends to follow closely behind. Make sure that you are neat and clean. Take the time to wash a stained shirt. Ask a godly friend to shop with you so you can have her opinion about what looks good on you and what doesn't. Wash your hair as often as needed to avoid excess oils. Lose some weight when it is needed.

Let me pause to say to anyone who battles a slow metabolism that I can relate. It has been a struggle to keep unwanted pounds away for as long as I can remember. It is hard work to eat healthy and exercise regularly. And I understand that there do exist medical conditions that make weight management arduous or even impossible. But when something can be done, it should be. (I do not like to hear it either, but it is important!) Extra pounds make being neat and orderly a more difficult task as clothing will not lie as nicely and will wrinkle more easily. If it is a problem for you, deal with your weight now as it will only become more difficult the older you get. And let me encourage you to get some help. It can seem very lonely if there is no one by your side to support you in your efforts. Ask your parents or a friend from church to keep you accountable in your weight goals. And certainly make it a matter of prayer, asking God to do in you what you do not have the power to do on your own. He is concerned about the details of your life — including your appearance.

I had a bag of carrots that spoiled long before their expiration date, and I brought them back to the grocery store for an exchange. The manager told me to just go pick out a new bag. Since there were some other items I needed as well, I went through the checkout line putting all my items on the belt except for the new bag of carrots. Knowing that the cashier was not aware of the situation, I said to him, "These carrots are an exchange that I already took care of up front — I don't want you thinking that I am trying to steal them." He replied, "I wasn't worried; I know you are not that type of person." Because we had never met before, I questioned him about his statement to which he replied, "You look like a church-going person; I can tell you would not lie." And in this case, his judgment was right on: I am a church going person, and I was not lying about the carrots. Why did he feel that he could trust me? What information did he have about me by which he could speculate that I went to church? Only my appearance! It may seem like a silly, insignificant story, but I was glad to know that my relationship with an orderly God was made obvious; for I do not want that truth to be camouflaged by a careless, sloppy appearance.

Camouflage Tactic #2 — Worldliness

A worldly, excessive consumption about your outward appearance will camouflage the truth that there is more to you than looks.

> *The life is more than meat, and the body is more than raiment. Consider the ravens: for they neither sow nor reap; which neither have storehouse nor barn; and God feedeth them: how much more are ye better than the fowls?...For all these things do the nations of the world seek after: and your Father knoweth that ye have need of these things. But rather seek ye the kingdom of God; and all these things shall be added unto you....For where your treasure is, there will your heart be also.* Luke 12:23-24, 30-31, 34

There is no question but that the world's focus is on temporal, material things. The world is consumed with money. The world is consumed with food. The world is consumed with clothing. But little concern does the world show for the kingdom of God. People do not care about the spiritual condition of their hearts. They do not grieve over sin that offends a holy, righteous God. They care only for themselves in the here and now. Unfortunately, even saved believers adopt much of this same worldly philosophy into their Christian lives. And it is a great hindrance to the cause of Christ. A believer who is consumed with the temporal things of this world is a poor testimony to that same world. And more specifically, a Christian who is consumed with maintaining a fashionable appearance sends a message to all those around her that looks are the most important thing to her and about her. The focus of a believer's life should be her relationship with God and her desire to be a witness to the lost souls around her. All of that is tragically jeopardized when one puts too much emphasis on appearance.

> *As a jewel of gold in a swine's snout, so is a fair woman which is without discretion.* Proverbs 11:22

Ever met someone who was physically beautiful but whose biblical understanding and character were lacking? If such a woman married, how would she help her husband? Would she be a submissive wife? Would she be wise in handling matters within the home? Would she be able to carry on a deep spiritual conversation with him? Would she know how to teach her children to live for God? Would she spend money wisely? Would her family call her blessed as the virtuous woman's family did? Would she be a good testimony to those in her church? Would she be burdened to win the lost to Christ? The sad answer to all these questions is: No! Her beauty would be of very little value to anyone. The point is that there are many things in a Christian's life that are of more importance than beauty.

Talking about wives, God instructs women as to what the focus of their lives should be.

> *Whose adorning let it not be that outward adorning of plaiting the hair, and of wearing of gold, or of putting on of apparel; But let it be the hidden man of the heart, in that which is not corruptible, even the ornament of a meek and quiet spirit, which is in the sight of God of great price.* I Peter 3:3-4

The point here is not that it is wrong for a woman to style her hair, put on jewelry, or wear clothes, but that she be focused more on the true adorning of herself by submission to God and her authorities.

> *In like manner also, that women adorn themselves in modest apparel, with shamefacedness and sobriety; not with broided hair, or gold, or pearls, or costly array; But (which becometh women professing godliness) with good works.*
> I Timothy 2:9-10

How is a woman to dress? Orderly, properly, and with moderation. The broided hair, gold, pearls, and costly array are all referring to an excessive, consuming relationship between a woman and her appearance. There is a difference between wearing a pair of earrings and a necklace that tastefully compliment an outfit and donning many huge rings and flashy chains worn to add flair. There is a difference between having neatly styled hair and spending much time and money to keep up with latest styles, many of which have the very purpose of drawing attention. But do not get sidetracked here from the main point of the passage—what truly becomes a woman goes beyond "skin deep." Godliness, good works, and submission are to be the focus of a Christian woman's life.

Have you been consumed with appearance? Do you feel like you never have enough money to spend on clothing, makeup, nails, and hair? Do you look down your nose at people who do not wear the acceptable name brands? Do you harbor feelings of jealousy because of someone else's natural beauty? Are you more concerned about how you look than you are about your relationship with the Lord? Do you sacrifice neatness and modesty for the sake of fashion? Do you make fun of other people who do not meet your fashion standards? Is the main activity of your life shopping? Do you pine about things you cannot change concerning your appearance (the shape of your nose, etc.)? Do you refuse to wear last year's styles because they are so out of date? Do you so respect beauty that you will not socialize with someone average looking? Do you feel pressure to head to the store if you see your friends are all wearing new outfits?

Perhaps this all sounds contradictory to camouflage tactic #1—carelessness and sloppiness. First I tell you to spend time and effort in making sure you look orderly and appropriate. And now I am telling you that it is wrong to focus your life on appearance. "Which is it?" you may ask. The answer is: YES! Both. There exists a right balance between making sure your appearance honors God and not allowing yourself to be consumed with looks. And that balance is not as hard to achieve as you might think. When someone strives to be neat and clean in order to honor God, the focus of that goal is pleasing God. When a person is consumed with how she looks, spending much time and money on making sure she keeps her hairstyle and clothing up to the world's standards, the focus of that goal is pleasing self.

Camouflage Tactic #3—Manliness

A masculine, tomboy attitude toward your outward appearance will camouflage the truth that you were created a female by God. That truth is not something about which to be ashamed. And it is not something that should be hidden. God created you to be female because He wanted you to be female. It would not have been better for you to be a man. And yet society puts pressure on girls to be tough like a guy, career-minded like a guy, and athletic like a guy. Rebellious, independent-minded women have the attitude that they can do anything as well as a man, if not better. My question is, Why the competition? Why do we as females want to be like men? A woman who thinks, acts, and dresses like a woman is not inferior to a man who thinks, acts, and dresses like a man. Nor is the man inferior to the woman. God created both. God loves both. God sent His Son to die for both. But we were created to be different. We are different.

> *So God created man in his own image, in the image of God created he him; male and female created he them.*
> Genesis 1:27

Male and *Female*, the names alone bear witness to that

difference. God created man to be a man! Made in the image of God, he was designed to be the leader, provider, and protector of the home.

> *God formed the woman out of the body of the man, not as an afterthought, but deliberately, to show her distinctive purpose and dependence on her husband.* (*Your Clothes Say It for You,* Elizabeth Rice Handford, pg. 37-38)

She was made for the man so that he would not be alone. She was made to be his help-meet.

> *Neither was the man created for the woman; but the woman for the man.* I Corinthians 11:9

That truth, however, does not make the women of less value than the man. In fact all throughout the Bible the woman who fears God is greatly esteemed.

> *Who can find a virtuous woman? for her price is far above rubies.* Proverbs 31:10

> *Whoso findeth a wife findeth a good thing, and obtaineth favour of the LORD.* Proverbs 18:22

> *A virtuous woman is a crown to her husband: but she that maketh ashamed is as rottenness in his bones.* Proverbs 12:4

> *But let it be the hidden man of the heart, in that which is not corruptible, even the ornament of a meek and quiet spirit, which is <u>in the sight of God of great price</u>.* I Peter 3:4

There exists no greater glory for a woman than for her to have the praise of God because she has submitted to and fulfilled His designed plan! Yet men and women alike are deceived into thinking that they need to erase the distinction. That does not please God; in fact it offends Him! Think about it: the created telling the Creator, "I do not like this male/female thing. I don't think there should be any difference. You did this wrong, and I am going to ignore such gender differentiation." How proud and rebellious to not accept what God made us to be! And that is exactly why God hates it when mankind takes upon themselves a unisex appearance.

> *The woman shall not wear that which pertaineth unto a man, neither shall a man put on a woman's garment: for all that do so are abomination unto the LORD thy God.*
> Deuteronomy 22:5

Something that is an abomination to God is always an abomination to Him! He loathes it when a man tries to assimilate a woman's appearance and begins to act effeminate refusing to take upon himself his God-given role of leadership. And God equally loathes it when a woman assumes upon herself the likeness of a man. She will also likely forsake her purpose, becoming assertive and independent, feeling compelled to compete and even conquer the male species. And furthermore, this perversion of God's distinction between the sexes promotes homosexuality.

Because that, when they knew God, they glorified him not as God, neither were thankful; but became vain in their imaginations, and their foolish heart was darkened....Who changed the truth of God into a lie, and worshipped and served the creature more than the Creator, who is blessed for ever. Amen. For this cause God gave them up unto vile affections: for even their women did change the natural use into that which is against nature: And likewise also the men, leaving the natural use of the woman, burned in their lust one toward another; men with men working that which is unseemly, and receiving in themselves that recompence of their error which was meet. Romans 1:21, 25-27

Such wickedness begins when people place mankind with his philosophies and ideas above God and His commands — including that of distinctive appearance.

What is it?
Much too frequently, my husband and I have had a little debate after being in a store, or restaurant, or walking down the street. We will pass by a person and my husband will whisper to me, "What was that? Was it a guy with shaggy hair or a girl with army pants and a brown boxy tee-shirt?"

"I think it was a guy. I cannot imagine any girl wearing an outfit like that and the way he stood was very manly," I would respond.

"I'm not so sure," he would say, "now that I think of it, I noticed she was wearing a nametag that said Kim."

Hmmmmm," would be all I could reply.

It is important—vitally important—that you accurately and clearly portray what you are: a female! You need to look and act feminine in every area of your life. Your actions and body language—the way you sit, stand, walk, and talk— should be ladylike. Your hair should not resemble that of a man's (I Corinthians 11:14-15), nor should your clothing be masculine. I think the easiest and best way to accomplish that while at the same time maintaining modesty is by not wearing pants. As I am out and about in my skirts or dresses, I am quite confident that people are able to make a very quick judgment about my gender. But I do not depend on skirts and dresses alone in my desire to look feminine. It is important that *every* part of my appearance gives testimony to the fact that I am a female.

From our back door, my husband and I were watching a handful of our summer staff riding horses. The distance was too far to see who any of the riders were, but one thing that we both noticed was how easy it was to tell the difference between the male and female riders. It was not because of a great difference in their riding ability as we had some young women who were nearly as talented as our main cowboy. And it was not because we could distinguish their faces. But the young women were distinctly feminine and the young men were obviously masculine in their appearance—so much so that there was no mistaking one for the other. When someone sees you out of the corner of his eye, or from a distance, he should immediately be able to tell "what you are."

What you wear reflects your attitude toward authority. It shows how you feel about being a woman. God wants your clothing (and overall appearance [author's note]) *to demonstrate that you gladly accept the position He has given you. Your clothing should plainly say, "I am a woman, and I gladly submit to God's will for my life."* (*Your Clothes Say It for You,* Elizabeth Rice Handford, pg. 55)

JOURNAL THOUGHTS

❑   I did not think that my appearance mattered to God, but I can now see that it does and that it is an important part of my testimony to the world around me.

❑   I have been guilty of camouflage tactic #1 by being careless or sloppy in my appearance, but I see the need to make these specific changes:

❑   I have been guilty of camouflage tactic #2 by being too consumed with my appearance, but I see the need to make these specific changes:

❑   I have been guilty of camouflage tactic #3 by not being feminine in every part of my appearance and need to make these specific changes:

CHAPTER TWELVE

Sticks and Stones

A mother and her young children were in the grocery store when one of them said in a voice loud enough for all to hear, "Mom, look at that guy! He has no legs!" Embarrassed, the mother tried to quiet the child. Young kids speak their minds.

After I taught a Wednesday night kids' club class in church, a girl came up to me with something obviously on her mind. "You look like the Grinch." She was not trying to be mean. She would have had no idea that such a comment could hurt my feelings. Because she simply thought it, she said it.

A grandchild on the floor was tracing with his finger the varicose veins on his grandmother's legs. "What are these things all over your legs, Grandma?" Kids can bring great humor into life. They do often say the funniest things. But what is spoken from an innocent young mouth ceases to be funny as that child grows.

When those little ones do not learn to control their tongues and continue to blurt out every thought that comes to their minds, they gain a reputation that is not good. It is even more unattractive to be in the company of a teen or an adult who has no control over her tongue. The tongue is a small part of the body, but it is mighty. In fact, it carries the brunt of the responsibility for our reputation.

My brethren, be not many masters, knowing that we shall receive the greater condemnation. For in many things we offend all. If any man offend not in word, the same is a perfect man, and able also to bridle the whole body. Behold, we put bits in the horses' mouths, that they may obey us; and we turn about their whole body. Behold also the ships, which though they be so great, and are driven of fierce winds, yet are they turned about with a very small helm, whithersoever the governor listeth. Even so the tongue is a little member, and boasteth great things. Behold, how great a matter a little fire kindleth! And the tongue is a fire, a world of iniquity: so is the tongue among our members, that it defileth the whole body, and setteth on fire the course of nature; and it is set on fire of hell. For every kind of beasts, and of birds, and of serpents, and of things in the sea, is tamed, and hath been tamed of mankind: But the tongue can no man tame; it is an unruly evil, full of deadly poison. Therewith bless we God, even the Father; and therewith curse we men, which are made after the similitude of God. Out of the same mouth proceedeth blessing and cursing. My brethren, these things ought not so to be.
James 3:1-10

Sticks and stones may break my bones, but words can never hurt me. We all know that this famous saying is far from true. When we think about words that hurt, we remember things said by *other people* that gave us pain. But rarely is any thought given to times when we hurt ourselves and our reputations with our *own* words.

Learning to control that small but fiery tongue is an important part of your preparation for the future. A wife who cannot control her tongue is unbearable. A mother who cannot control her tongue brings great devastation to her home. A friend who cannot control her tongue is no friend at all. A church member who cannot control her tongue brings shame to the whole congregation. Your tongue affects today. Your tongue affects your future. It is so important that you learn to control it now.

20,000 Words a Day

It is said that a female speaks 20,000 words a day which is three times more than the average male. A husband tells a joke that goes: "I don't mean to imply that my wife talks too much, but she went to the beach and came back with a sunburned tongue." In general, women hold the reputation of being more talkative than men. My parents told me of an older couple they were visiting for an afternoon. The wife talked and talked and talked. It seemed the husband did not have much to say. But then he invited my father to the basement for a look around. Once in the basement, away from the wife, the husband talked and talked. He had plenty to say but could never get in a word as long as his wife was there. While there certainly are exceptions, women tend to enjoy talking. We can spend hours on the phone. We e-mail often. The minutes can go by so quickly when chatting with a favorite friend. While it is not wrong for a person to become involved in a conversation, it is interesting what the Bible says about much talk.

He that hath knowledge spareth his words: and a man of understanding is of an excellent spirit. Even a fool, when he holdeth his peace, is counted wise: and he that shutteth his lips is esteemed a man of understanding. Proverbs 17:27-28

These verses remind me of the saying that goes something like this: *It is better to keep silent and be considered a fool than to open your mouth and remove all doubt.* There have been times I could have saved myself embarrassment if I had shut my lips instead of opening them.

We were entertaining a visiting preacher and his wife in our home for the noon meal. It was mentioned that we had recently had a building burglarized. The preacher had also had some problems with burglary in his church years ago. Stories turned into more stories. My mind was spinning with police, robbers, and crimes when my cell phone rang. I stepped into another room to answer. "Hello." "Hello." No one answered, but I could hear noise coming from the other end. I listened carefully and suddenly realized I was hearing the conversation from the dining room through my cell phone. My mind raced. Someone had bugged my house and called me! Now I was hearing this bug through my phone. I quickly went back to the kitchen, handed my husband the phone, and said, "Listen to this. Someone has bugged our conversation."

My husband listened for a minute, looked down at his belt, picked up his cell phone, and said, "I accidentally called you. You could hear the conversation from my phone." I was so embarrassed. I definitely opened my mouth and *removed all doubt.*

While this story and other similar ones can be humorous, many times our words bring reproach instead of laughs. Each time we open our mouths, we establish more of a reputation—either to the good or bad. That day I gave myself the reputation of being a little air-headed. It would have been more regrettable, however, to have given myself the reputation of being a busy-body always needing to know everything that is happening with other people; a proud know-it-all person who shares speculations as fact; or an untrustworthy friend who cannot keep personal matters personal. We could avoid such reputations if we would heed the advice of Proverbs. A wise person spares his words. Even a fool, who speaks few words instead of speaking his mind with constant talk, will be seen by others as wise. It would do you good to learn this now. It does not mean you can never enjoy good conversation with friends. But it encourages us to make the habit of our life to shut our lips instead of opening them. It is implied here that we think before we speak. It is also implied that we do not speak everything we think. We have been teaching this truth to our children. "Just because you think it, doesn't mean you have to say it" is a frequent phrase we quote in our home. I know there are times I spew out words almost faster than my thoughts are formed. That is not wise. Often it causes grief to either me or others and most often both. Learn to think before you speak. When you do, you will find you have less to say.

> *In the multitude of words there wanteth not sin: but he that refraineth his lips is wise.* Proverbs10:19

> *He that keepeth his mouth keepeth his life: but he that openeth wide his lips shall have destruction.* Proverbs 13:3

> *Whoso keepeth his mouth and his tongue keepeth his soul from troubles.* Proverbs 21:23

> *A fool uttereth all his mind: but a wise man keepeth it in till afterwards.* Proverbs 29:11

Lots of talk tends toward lots of sin and trouble. Many words often include pride, gossip, stretching the truth, unkindness, rudeness, griping, and even unintentionally hurting others. It is wise to restrain your lips. So many women did not learn to do this as girls and teens, and now they speak foolishness constantly.

My husband and I were visiting with a lady in her sixties. We learned much about her in the short time we were with her. She did not restrain her lips. She showed her bitterness by telling a story about her former husband. Her pride was made evident by her words as well. It seemed she had a strong opinion about everything—the type of opinion that was "always right." She did not speak kindly of others. She complained much. Having our ears full, we were glad to leave. I could not help but wonder what unkind words and opinions were said about us after we left. The trouble, sin, and destruction that came from this woman's lips did not start in her sixties. I feel confident it could be traced back much further. Now is the time to tame your talk. Spare your words.

That Smarts!

We were eating and enjoying our dinner when all of a sudden my daughter cried out loudly in pain. "What's the matter? What's the matter?" I asked, concerned. In a muffled slur, she answered that she had bit her tongue. And quite a bite she had taken. After the bleeding stopped, you could see where her teeth had ripped the flesh open. OUCH! While the literal biting of the tongue can be excruciating, if we do not learn to bite our tongues in several specific areas, we may inflict great pain as well.

Bite the tongue of cursing.

Swearing, cursing, taking God's name in vain, and all other types of foul language are wrong. This type of talk should never come out of the mouth of any believer in Christ. Our talk needs to show other people that we are Christians. It should be different from the talk of the world. Our talk also needs to show that we are ladies. Cursing and swearing is never ladylike. Many women speak crudely to emphasize the fact they are trying to be like one of the guys. It is not right for a female to try to dress, talk, or act like a male. Furthermore, it is wrong for a man to speak foully. If it is wrong for men, then it certainly is wrong for women.

> *Thou shalt not take the name of the LORD thy God in vain; for the LORD will not hold him guiltless that taketh his name in vain.* Exodus 20:7

This verse and others clearly forbid the use of God's name in any improper way. Using the name of God, Christ, Jesus, or any abbreviated form of God's name is wrong. We should never use God's name lightly. And we should never use it as a curse word. Maybe you have gotten into the bad habit of this. Habits are hard to break, but you need to break this one. Start by recognizing the "habit" as sin. Be angry at this sin. Confess it. Ask God to give you victory in it. Then think about your every word. Catch yourself before the wickedness can escape your mouth. If you slip up, confess the sin again. Keep after yourself until the habit is broken and the temptation no longer lures you. Visualize that foul language as a terrible spider on your shoulder. Do not rest until that spider is dead and gone.

There is other foul language besides taking the Lord's name in vain. Peter used it when he denied knowing Jesus.

> *And after a while came unto him they that stood by, and said to Peter, Surely thou also art one of them; for thy speech bewrayeth thee. Then began he* [Peter] *to curse and to swear,*

saying, I know not the man. And immediately the cock crew.
Matthew 26:73-74

We do not know what curse words Peter used. The specific
words are not the emphasis. But there were specific words
in that day, in that country, in that language, and in that
culture that were known to be curse words. There are in
our day, in our country, in our language, and in our culture
words that are known to be curse words. Peter used cursing
and swearing to lie about himself and to try to prove that he
was not associated with Christ. So often Christians use the
foul language just as Peter did—lying about themselves in
an effort to prove they are not Christ's followers. They want
to fit in with the crowd—an unbelieving crowd. Peter wept
bitterly because of his sin that involved cursing. We should
also have a bitter hatred for it.

Bite the tongue of lying.
It can be a great temptation. "A little white lie" can get
you out of trouble. A little exaggeration can make telling
the story fun. Stretching the truth can keep you from being
humiliated in front of others. Lying can keep your pride
from getting hurt. What ever the reasoning behind it, there
is constant temptation to lie. But it is wrong; it is sin.

I have never thought that I was a liar. But after reading
several verses that emphasized how God abhors lying, I
decided to examine myself to make sure. For several days I
paid close attention to every word I spoke, asking myself if
there was even the slightest untruth. It was not long before
I caught myself. It was just a little stretch of the truth that

came out to protect my pride. I was surprised, disappointed, and warned. I was a liar and susceptible to its temptation. That examination was helpful to me. Since then I have been able to recognize and refuse the temptation to lie before the words spilt out of my mouth. Lying is very deceiving—so deceiving, in fact, that it not only fools others, but fools us into believing it as well. Do not assume you are not guilty without a prayerful self-examination. You too may be surprised.

Lying lips are abomination to the LORD: but they that deal truly are his delight. Proverbs 12:22

Bite the tongue of gossip.

He that goeth about as a talebearer revealeth secrets: therefore meddle not with him that flattereth with his lips.
Proverbs 20:19

A talebearer is someone who loves to tell news—juicy news. Whether the story is true or not, the talebearer so enjoys sharing it. While women are the ones often accused of gossip, the talebearer I have had to deal with the most is a man. This man is very cunning in his tale telling. In fact, it took my husband and me several years of conversations with him before we recognized it. He does love to tell stories—stories about other people. And some of those stories are hilarious. That is why it took us so long to recognize the problem—we were too busy laughing. But after a while we realized that his stories put the person about whom it was told in a bad light. This talebearer would tell and laugh. And we would listen and laugh. But now we have stopped laughing, for each story cunningly cuts down another believer. Each story has a theme of, "Can you believe so and so—he is a real dummy!" We have also seen in this talebearer the tendency toward flattery. He says things that make us feel good. He builds us up. My husband and I have concluded the reason for this. The flattery brings a comfort level. Feeling comfortable, we are more likely to talk and share with him. While talking and sharing, we are giving him more gossip ammunition—ammunition that can later be used to tell stories about *us*. I feel confident that not only have we heard some of his stories, but also have been the real dummies in stories told to other people.

Proverbs makes this connection between flattery and talebearing. While talebearers may be interesting, popular, and funny, we are warned to stay away from them. Perhaps in the description of my talebearing acquaintance, you have seen a little of yourself. Women certainly can be and are involved in talebearing. Do not repeat stories that are juicy. Do not be the one who is known for saying, "Did you hear?" Do not pride yourself in putting others in a bad light—even if it is funny. Be a dependable friend. Unless there is need to get help in dealing with a dangerous or sinful situation, you do not need to blab things your friends or parents have confided in you. This is important concerning your preparation for the future.

A woman who is a talebearer has a husband who cannot trust her. He cannot share with her his thoughts, his concerns, or his prayers because he knows that she will not keep them private. He will not want to tell her about a hard time he is going through for fear the whole church will know about it. He will weary of her telling her parents everything he does and says. It will cause a strain in the marriage. It is wrong to be a gossiper, and it will hinder God's best for your life.

Bite the tongue of unkindness.

This one is a little ironic because an unkind tongue is biting.

> *There is that speaketh like the piercings of a sword: but the tongue of the wise is health.* Proverbs 12:18

How often I have heard mouths of brothers and sisters pierce like a sword. The verbal battle that can go on between two sisters can match the fierceness of war. The words flung from the tongue of one schoolmate to another stab deep. The opinions of one church member are hurled like darts at another. Words, like sticks and stones, can hurt.

> *But the tongue can no man tame....Therewith bless we God, even the Father; and therewith curse we men, which are made after the similitude of God. Out of the same mouth proceedeth blessing and cursing. My brethren, these things ought not so to be.* James 3:8a, 9-10

Your tongue has the ability to be unkind, and an unkind tongue destroys relationships. As it lashes out against your sister, your mother, or your friend, it causes them great harm and severs the closeness between you. In the future, it will cause unnecessary conflict in the home. If you speak unkindly now, do you think that habit will stop if God allows you to marry? No. Your fiery tongue will eventually strike out upon your husband and your children as well. Now is the time to deal with your piercing mouth. Now is the time to confess it as sin and hate it.

Be careful about joking with meanness. Young people are known for their jovial, yet mean bantering. "Where did *you* learn to drive?" "You moron!" "Did someone pinch your nose with a pair of pliers or is that a pimple?" While the intentions of the humor may be innocent, the person bearing the brunt of the joke is likely hurt by it. Maybe you are a person who can take it without being offended. Be glad for that. At the same time realize that others may be more sensitive.

You can easily be guilty of speaking unkindly about a person without ever talking directly to them. Talking negatively *about* people to other people is so common that most of the time we think nothing of it. In fact, you can be a very nice mean person. Perhaps you would never consider speaking unkindly *to* someone, but you say mean things *about* them. It is called backbiting—talking unkindly about other people when they are not there. It happens much too often. Unfortunately, it is an accepted behavior. We have likely all been guilty of it. To my shame, I know I have. But the fact that it is an accepted behavior in our culture, even our Christian culture, does not make it right.

LORD, who shall abide in thy tabernacle? who shall dwell in thy holy hill? He that walketh uprightly, and worketh

*righteousness, and speaketh the truth in his heart. He that
backbiteth not with his tongue, nor doeth evil to his neighbor,
nor taketh up a reproach against his neighbor.* Psalm 15:1-3

Speak not evil one of another, brethren. James 4:11a

I have some friends that I highly respect and trust primarily
because I have not heard them speak negatively about
others. It is obvious that they have made a decision to not
be guilty of backbiting. It makes them good friends. I do not
wonder if they are talking behind my back. I know others,
however, who have often tickled my ears with negative
comments about other people. It makes me uncomfortable
being around them because of their verbal bashing of others.
It also makes me wonder what they say about me behind
my back. I do not trust them. I do not want to spend a lot
of time with them. And most of all, I do not want to be like
them. I need to hate the sin of backbiting making sure I am
not guilty of it. And so do you. It is a sin that can easily slip
by. It is easy not to notice it. Sift every word you are about
to speak through a mental test. Is it kind? Does it build up
or tear down? Is it backbiting? Should it be said?

It continually amazes me how many women backbite their
own husbands. Women get together and seem to think it
is all right to talk negatively about their mates. The wives
bond together. They all understand what it is like to be
married to a lazy, sloppy bum. They like to talk about it,
and they like the bond. It is a wicked, rebellious bond. A
wife ought never to be found guilty of word-bashing her
husband — even if he really is a bum! He is her husband,

and she ought to speak respectfully not only *to* him, but also *of* him. Though marriage may be off in the future, make the decision now that if God gives you a husband you will never speak negatively about him. You will not complain to your mother about him. You will not take part in the husband bashing bond. You will only speak kindly of him. If only women understood how much harm they do to both their husbands and marriages by their backbiting! It is devastating.

> *Be kindly affectioned one to another with brotherly love; in honour preferring one another.* Romans 12:10

Bite the complaining tongue.

One of the challenging jobs as a junior camp counselor at the Bill Rice Ranch is dealing with complainers. While most of the kids love the week of camp, it seems there is always that one who does not enjoy anything. "Do we have to play that?" "It is soooooo hot. I think I am going to die of thirst." "I want to go swimming right now." "My mom didn't give me enough money." "I don't like pizza." Being around that type of junior camper is frustrating. Being around that type of teen or adult is even more frustrating. Everything seems negative. They never seem happy or content with their work, their church, their family, their home, their location, or their friends. "Things should have been done differently," complainers say. While you may or may not be such a chronic complainer, any complaining is wrong. I have recently memorized a verse to remind myself of what God thinks of it.

And when the people complained, it displeased the LORD: and the LORD heard it; and his anger was kindled.
Numbers 11:1a

The children of Israel were known for their complaining. They complained when they saw the Egyptian army pursuing them and fussed at Moses for bringing them out of the land. They complained about the lack of food. They complained about the lack of water. They complained because they missed the food they had back when they were slaves in Egypt. They had seen God deliver and provide for them time and time again. Yet instead of seeking God about their needs and thanking Him for provision, they complained. Whether the complaining spirit be against God or man, it is wrong and it displeases God.

Do all things without murmurings and disputings.
Philippians 2:14

Have your parents made a rule? Do not murmur about it. Is there an activity in your youth group that seems boring? Do not gripe about it. Are you given a job to do? Do not displease God by complaining. Is the meal set before you something you do not care for? Be thankful for the food and for the one who took time to prepare it. Still have some years of school left? Do not fuss about it. Do everything you do without complaining, fussing, muttering, griping. It is all the same thing—murmuring.
If you do not drive that complaining spirit away now, you will become a murmuring wife, mother, friend, co-worker, church member, citizen, and neighbor. Who can bear being

in the presence of a complainer? Only another complainer!

Bite the self-centered tongue.

Have you ever been around a person that talked about themselves so much that you wished you had a mute button? On and on she goes, never seeming interested in anything you might have to say. After a while you find yourself avoiding her. Why? It is because she is self-centered. I have heard it said that if you are having trouble conversing with someone that you do not know well, get her talking about herself and you will have an easy (one-way) conversation. People do love talking about their own interests, their own abilities, their own family, their own experiences, and their own opinions. I am not suggesting that you never talk about things that interest you, but I do suggest you take a moment to reflect on your conversations. Do you talk much more than you listen? Has your purpose primarily been to promote yourself or the other person? Do you frequently interrupt with your thoughts?

I have a friend who is a very sociable person. It seems she can carry on a good conversation with just about anybody. Being a fairly quiet person myself, I have admired this ability in her. After spending some time with her, I realized that she did not talk about herself much. Almost all her conversations begin with a question. "Where have you been lately?" "How are your kids doing in school?" "Where are you spending Christmas?" Then she listens *with interest* to the answers. It is no wonder people enjoy talking with her. You and I both can learn from her example.

Bite the contentious tongue.

My husband was away; the kids were asleep; and I had finally landed in bed after a tiring day. I was just starting to relax when… drip… drip… drip… drip… drip. Not wanting to leave the warm, comfy bed, I tried to ignore it. Drip… drip… drip… drip. The more I tried to block it out, the louder and more annoying it seemed. Drip… drip… drip… drip… drip. Ugggghh! I got up, tightened the knobs on the shower, and settled back down in bed. Silence. Then Drip. Drip… drip… drip… drip… drip. A constant drip is enough to drive the most patient person crazy. In fact, I have heard that in times past the Chinese used dripping water as part of their prison torture. Living with a contentious woman causes a man the same type of unbearable annoyance.

A continual dropping in a very rainy day and a contentious woman are alike. Proverbs 27:15

It is better to dwell in a corner of the housetop, than with a brawling woman in a wide house. Proverbs 21:9

A foolish son is the calamity of his father: and the contentions of a wife are a continual dropping. Proverbs 19:13

I hope you can see already how biting this tongue is important to your preparation for the future. The Bible shows pity on a man that must live with such a woman by declaring it would be better for him to dwell on the roof. A woman who constantly picks, picks, picks is not a good wife. The contentious woman enjoys causing strife. She looks for faults and is always bothered. She is easily angered and disgusted. She scolds in her unhappiness.

Have you ever heard the expression, "If Mamma ain't happy, ain't nobody happy"? Hollywood often takes that unhappy, contentious Mamma and makes a funny storyline out of her. "Yes, Dear" are the only words her husband uses because he knows better than to say anything else. In a fictitious setting, it can be very funny. But it is far from funny in real life. Because the description of the contentious woman is drastically negative, you and I probably would never naturally compare ourselves to her. But there have been times in my home when this Mamma was not happy. And, well…need I say more?

We may be guilty of being contentious women much more than we realize. Before marriage, perhaps the easiest relationship to examine is the one with brothers and sisters. You are likely to have more contention with them than with anyone else. Are you constantly feeding that contention? Do you pick, pick, pick? Are you involved in frequent bickering? Do you provoke that brother or sister? Do you often scold and correct them? If you were truly honest with yourself, would you admit that you even enjoy the strife? Are you easily bothered by them? Do you boss them? Do you become upset when you do not get your way? When you are not happy, do you make sure they are not happy either? If you do not have brothers or sisters, ask these same questions concerning close friends or roommates. If the answers to any of these questions is "yes" and you do not begin dealing with the problem now, your future husband will want to make sure he has a sturdy roof on the house, because he will be spending a lot of time up there. Do not deceive yourself into thinking you would not treat your husband that same way. How you speak to your parents, siblings, and friends now is most likely how you will speak to your husband if and when you have one. Bite that contentious tongue now so you will know how to bite it in the future as well.

Bite the rash tongue.

> *He that answereth a matter before he heareth it, it is folly and shame unto him.* Proverbs 18:13

It is so important to learn to listen to the whole story before responding. We tend to assume we know what the other person is thinking. We assume we know when the other person is angry. We assume we know exactly how the other person feels. We assume we know what happened. We assume, and we answer. And it does end in folly and shame. I could not count on my fingers the times I have caused conflict in my marriage because I assumed. I did not wait to find out what he was really thinking or what really happened. I thought I knew, and I answered. What unnecessary heartache my rashness has caused! Answering a matter before hearing it can cause problems in all relationships: in marriage, with parents, with children, with friends, with neighbors, with brothers and sisters, with co-workers, with teachers, and with church members.

> *Wherefore, my beloved brethren, let every man be swift to hear, slow to speak, slow to wrath: For the wrath of man worketh*

not the righteousness of God. James 1:19-20

Slow down your tongue, and use the extra time to listen.

She Opened Her Mouth

"My only hope is to never say another word," you may be thinking after reading about all the tongues we need to bite. "If a person who restrains her lips is wise, should I ever open mine?" Obviously, we cannot and should not go through life refusing to speak. While it is hard enough trying to avoid saying the wrong thing, I think it can be even more difficult trying to figure out the right thing to say. Thankfully, the virtuous woman gives us a good example to follow.

> *She openeth her mouth with wisdom; and in her tongue is the law of kindness.* Proverbs 31:26

The right words are always wise words.
Notice that she did open her mouth to speak but made sure the words that came forth were right words. She spoke with wisdom. She held the reins of her tongue tightly by checking them through wisdom. At first this sounds complicated and impossible, yet it is actually very simple. Wisdom is available to anyone who wants it. Listen to Wisdom speaking in Proverbs:

> *I love them that love me; and those that seek me early shall find me.* Proverbs 8:17

All throughout the book of Proverbs, Wisdom is given a voice that says, "I am here, and I am ready to give myself to anyone who seeks me and wants to be instructed by me."

Give instruction to a wise man, and he will be yet wiser.
Proverbs 9:9a

Receiving instruction is the key to receiving wisdom. The Bible is an instruction book. Wisdom and the Word of God go hand in hand. A person cannot have true wisdom apart from the Bible.

O how love I thy law! it is my meditation all the day. Thou through thy commandments hast made me wiser than mine enemies: for they are ever with me. I have more understanding than all my teachers: for thy testimonies are my meditation. I understand more than the ancients, because I keep thy precepts. Psalm 119:97-100

The psalmist was wise, not because of intellect or personality, but because he chose to receive instruction from God's Word. In fact, he sought it. He loved it. And God gave him wisdom.

If thou seekest her as silver, and searchest for her as for hid treasures; Then shalt thou understand the fear of the LORD, and find the knowledge of God. For the LORD giveth wisdom: out of his mouth cometh knowledge and understanding.
Proverbs 2:4-6

If you lack wisdom, perhaps it is because you are not seeking and receiving instruction from the Word of God. Or perhaps it is because you are not asking for it.

If any of you lack wisdom, let him ask of God, that giveth to all men liberally, and upbraideth not; and it shall be given him.
James 1:5

We can ask God for the wisdom we need in any situation including those concerning our words and conversations. It is when we do not ask God to guide our mouths that we spew out foolish things. It is when we give no thought to His Word that we also give no thought to the importance of our tongue. I have experienced both sides. I can clearly remember words and conversations about which I gave no regard to God and His instruction. I did not ask for wisdom. I did not ask Him to keep me from saying anything unkind or hurtful. I just spoke. I certainly did not open my mouth with wisdom. I wish I could take back those words spoken without God's help, but I cannot. And it did affect my reputation. On the other hand, there have been times I sought God before entering into a conversation. I reminded myself of Proverbs and the benefit of speaking sparingly. On those occasions I received definite help from God and the wisdom of His Word. It has caused me to realize that every word and conversation is important—no matter how insignificant the topic seems. It has burned a desire in my heart to ask God for help before every conversation. How wonderful a change there would be if you and I did just that!

The right words are always kind words.
Have you ever had your day brightened by a kind word? Maybe a friend complimented your hair. Maybe your pastor's wife pointed out that she could see the spiritual growth taking place in your life. Maybe you got some verbal encouragement from your mom after a hard day. Whatever the kindness, it lifted your heart. I will never forget a pastor's kind words of encouragement sent through an e-mail. We received it at a time of great hardship and discouragement. It was the only kind thing that had been said to us for weeks during a time we had been pouring everything into a ministry full of people. Those short words of kindness helped carry me through a difficult time. They brought cheer to my day. They meant so much to me. Having received words of kindness that lightened my day, I have had the desire to be the one who cheers the day of another person. Really, it is not that hard of a thing to do, yet often we do not. Perhaps it is because we get so busy and self-centered that it never enters our mind to say a word for the benefit of another person. Make it a goal today to brighten someone's day with a kind word and begin making it a habit.

In the tongue of the virtuous woman was the law of kindness. She was both the law maker and law enforcer for her tongue, and she strove to keep it from getting out of control by frequently testing it. Often in construction zones, the police set a little computerized machine in the road that displays for you the speed at which you are currently traveling. Its job is to remind you that your speed needs to match the posted speed limit. It wants you to say, "Oh, am I really going that fast? I'd better slow down." I picture the virtuous woman putting every word she is about to speak into a similar machine. But instead of a number, this machine blinks out a message that will determine whether she will open her mouth or not. If she reads "kind," then she can proceed with caution. But if she reads "unkind," she ought to slow down and reevaluate her thoughts before they escape her mouth. Using this kindness test gave her a reputation—one so good that it was written about in God's Word so that we would have an example to follow.

Their Reputations Live On

Polly Gore was one of the sweetest, most cheerful old ladies I have ever met. I will not soon forget her funeral. It was not a large chapel, but it was full—full of people whose lives had been touched by Miss Polly's. Several heads, including mine, nodded in agreement during the service when it was mentioned that Miss Polly never complained. To ask her about her failing health was to see a sparkle come to her eye as she said, "I'm just trusting the Lord." During her stays at the hospital, she would ask her pastor to bring her more gospel tracts because she had given all hers out having already witnessed to several nurses. I remember times when Miss Polly had called me just to find out how our ministry was doing. As I sat at that funeral, I could not help but think, "I want to be like Miss Polly." Sometime in her life she had learned to bite the negative tongue and replace it with a kind and loving one. And while her body lay there cold and lifeless, her reputation did not. It lived and does live on.

I could not be at the funeral of Mrs. Gen Purple, but I imagine it similar to the one of Polly Gore—filled with people with only positive thoughts. For Mrs. Purple too was a sweet lady. Her tongue was filled with kindness. She took an interest in others, not herself. In ten years of knowing her, I never heard her complain, gossip, or say anything unkind. She was quiet, but not shy. Sometime in her life she had learned to spare her words, thinking before she spoke, making sure there was no sin rolling off her tongue. The result—an incredible testimony. Often I have thought, "I want to be like Mrs. Purple." Her body lies in the grave, but her reputation does not. It lives on.

It is time for your funeral to start. What will be in the minds of those attending? Will the preacher have had to think a long time to come up with a positive comment? Will people remember you as a sweet lady who never complained? Or will they be thinking about the many times you spoke negatively about others? Will they be able to say you took an interest in them, or will they be embarrassed to say anything because you were a self-promoting person? Will they remember the time you brightened their day with a kind word or the times you always seemed to emphasize their faults? Will anyone there be thinking, "I want to be like…"? You see, your tongue affects your reputation—for the good or for the bad. May all of us strive to be like Miss Polly and Mrs. Purple.

JOURNAL THOUGHTS

❑   I have had a cursing tongue. (List specific instances.)

❑   I have had a lying tongue. (List specific instances.)

❑   I have had a gossiping tongue. (List specific instances.)

❑   I have had an unkind tongue. (List specific instances.)

❑   I have had a complaining tongue.
(List specific instances.)

❑   I have had a self-centered tongue.
(List specific instances.)

❑   I have had a contentious tongue.
(List specific instances.)

❑   I have had a rash tongue. (List specific instances.)

❑   I am also confessing to God my sin in the areas I
marked above.

❑   I can think of these specific steps that I can take to help
me in my desire to bite these sinful tongues:

❑   I realize that my tongue plays a great role in my reputation. I want to learn to put my words through a kindness
test and ask God for wisdom in my conversations.

CHAPTER THIRTEEN
Chasing Butterflies

Megan was five, and she desperately wanted a pet. She would be pleased with any number of animals — a dog, a cat, a horse, a rabbit, a bird. Because it seemed like she would have to wait forever, she was determined to find herself a pet. Everywhere Megan went, she kept her eyes open. One warm summer afternoon while playing outside, she spotted the most beautiful butterfly. The chase began. She ran this way and that way with her arms stretched up trying to grasp it. At each swipe, that butterfly fluttered up or down or to the side just out of Megan's reach. After several attempts, she ran to the garage, dug through her toy box, and pulled out a small play net. As fast as her little legs would carry her, she sprinted back to the front lawn. She stopped and gazed all around. Not by the tree. Not in the flower bed. Not over the driveway. Not by the fence. Not on the porch. Nowhere. The butterfly was gone. She sat down on the grass with the little net resting across her knees. Then the silent tears began, interrupted only by a quiet sniff or two.

Losing a butterfly may seem insignificant to you, but it was not to Megan. She felt her heart sink. She felt that choking lump in her throat. She thought her desire for a pet was hopeless. She felt crushed. Those emotions were all very real to her. While you may not burst into tears over an insect, your emotions are very real to you as well. In fact, it may seem that you are always chasing emotional butterflies. Those emotions run this way then that way, unpredictably all over the place. Can there exist any stability? Is there Bible help in dealing with emotions? Thankfully, there is.

It Is Good

It is easy to become frustrated at emotions. Sometimes they seem to be the reason for all our troubles. I have several times wished I could get rid of my feelings forever. In fact, there was one time I clearly remember declaring war on my emotions. I was so tired of their existence that I decided I wanted to annihilate them altogether. So I set out to become emotionless. I was going to be cool, calm and undaunted. On the outside, I was relatively successful. I showed little sign of any emotion. But I was not only miserable on the inside; I was a miserable person to live with. I was hard and insensitive. After it was all said and done, my husband begged me to never declare war on my emotions again. He said he would much rather deal with the occasional tears than the misery without them. A war fought against emotions with the intention of destroying them will not be won. There is no success in trying to battle against feelings using other feelings as ammunition. The first key to having emotional stability in your life is to realize that emotions are not your enemy.

So God created man in his own image, in the image of God created he him; male and female created he them....And God saw every thing that he had made, and, behold, it was very good. Genesis 1:27, 31a

When God created us, both men and women, He created us as emotional beings. Those emotions were a part of "very good." It is true that when sin entered the world, emotions along with everything else became scarred. Emotions certainly can be sinful. While sin is an enemy, being an emotional creature is not. God created us that way. And He created male and female. There are many differences between the two including emotional makeup. I have met some outwardly emotional men and some outwardly unemotional women. Typically, however, females are more emotional. God has created women with an extra sensitivity. That tenderness is one of the things that attracts the attention of the man. My husband likes it that my emotional makeup makes me fragile and in need of a protector. And he wants to be my protector. It would be unattractive and unnatural to both of us if it were the other way around.

Another reason God gave women an extra dose of sensitivity is so they could fill the role of mother.

Can a woman forget her sucking child, that she should not have compassion on the son of her womb? yea, they may forget, yet will I not forget thee. Isaiah 49:15

This verse reveals God's love. When Israel thought God had forgotten her, He points out that His love exceeds all human love. Can a woman forget her tiny, helpless baby? Is a woman capable of turning her ears away from the cries of her own child? While the sad answer is — "yes," it is unusual. A mother's compassion for the cry of her own baby is great. Because we cannot comprehend God's compassion, He illustrates using the greatest compassion known to man — the compassion of a mother. That tenderness is God-given. That sensitivity is purposefully designed and very good.

Being an emotional creature is not bad. Do not fight it. Do not harden yourself to it. It is not wrong for tears to roll occasionally. The goal must not be to get rid of all feelings but to get those feelings where they belong.

Follow the Leader

Do you remember how the game goes? The leader is in front of the line and all the other kids follow behind mimicking him. If the leader jumps, then the followers jump too. If the leader swings his arms, the followers swing their arms as well. When playing the game, you always want to make sure the right kid gets the job of leader because he determines the game. If he is boring and cannot think of anything exciting to do, then everyone suffers. But if he is imaginative, he can make it fun for everyone. In your life, you have a will, and you have emotions; both are needed. But "the game" does not go well if the wrong one gets the job of leader. Instability comes when you say to emotions, "It's your turn to be leader; I will follow you." You will then be chasing emotional butterflies. You go here, no there, back that way again, up and over, upside down, and everywhere. You see, having emotions is not the problem; allowing them to lead is. The spot for emotions in your life is as the follower.

Commit thy works unto the LORD, and thy thoughts shall be established. Proverbs 16:3

Committing your works unto the Lord is primary and should be the leading force in your life. Thoughts or feelings or emotions should follow. It is when the two switch places and you allow yourself to be led around by your feelings that you get into trouble and become unstable. Rachel and Leah both allowed their emotions to take the lead in their lives, and it resulted in a silly soap opera-type experience. Jacob loved Rachel, but he was tricked into marrying Leah who was less than beautiful. Stuck with Leah, he decided to marry Rachel as well. Two sisters married to one man! The Bible says that because Leah was hated, God had compassion on her and opened her womb. She had four sons. That made Rachel very unhappy. In her turmoil, Rachel went to Jacob and said:

Give me children, or else I die. Genesis 30:1b

How dramatic! Rachel was chasing butterflies; she allowed her feelings (many of which were sinful in this case) to lead her life.

And she said, Behold my maid Bilhah, go in unto her; and she shall bear upon my knees, that I may also have children by her. And she gave him Bilhah her handmaid to wife. Genesis 30:3-4a

It is as if Rachel were saying, "Okay, Jacob, since you and God will not give me children, I will get some on my own. You take my servant and make her your wife, and the children that she has will be mine." Sounds crazy, doesn't it? Well it gets more complicated when Leah joins the butterfly party. After Rachel's servant had two sons, Leah became concerned. She had not had any more children and thought maybe Rachel would catch up to her. She took Zilpah her maid, and gave her to Jacob to wife. That maid had two sons for Leah.

And Leah said, Happy am I, for the daughters will call me blessed. Genesis 30:13a

With the addition of more children, Leah probably did feel happy for a while. But that happiness did not last because Rachel bore more sons as well. Both sisters, led by their emotions, went up and down, this way and that, topsy-turvy and all around. They allowed their thoughts to control them and did not follow the truth of Proverbs 16:3. What a mess!

Another example is the instance King Ahab coveted a vineyard. Because it was perfect for planting the garden of herbs he wanted, he tried to buy the vineyard from Naboth, the owner. But the land was a family inheritance, and Naboth did not want to sell it. King Ahab was distraught.

All he could think about was that vineyard. He was in such turmoil that he would not even eat. His thoughts and feelings consumed his life. His wife plotted to have Naboth falsely accused and killed. The king consented and got just what he wanted—the vineyard. But he went so far as to kill a man for it. He was led by his feelings. He did not commit his way unto the Lord and allow his thoughts to follow. He placed those thoughts into leadership. Again, what a mess!

Remember Elijah's pity party? The queen hated him because she hated the God he served and was seeking to kill him. Elijah went and hid himself in a cave and whined to God that he was all alone. It is true that Elijah's circumstances were hard and that the future looked bleak. But even in the midst of difficult times, Elijah should have committed his works unto the Lord. Instead, he allowed his feelings to lead.

Oh, the unnecessary heartache that is caused when emotions lead! Our emotional life will be stable as long as it is following. If we allow our thoughts to take the lead, then we are in trouble. Commit your works unto the Lord and your thoughts will come along behind. Your emotions will be where they should be. Feelings follow—or should follow. Learn to commit your works to the Lord by putting three leaders out in front of the game.

Be led by what you know not by what you feel.
This can easily be illustrated in assurance of salvation. If I allow my feelings to lead, then I will likely have doubts about my salvation. That is because there are times that

I do not "feel" saved. There are days when I do not feel emotionally well. I may feel down and sad. If I allow those feelings to lead, then I likely may say, "I must not even be saved. Christians are not supposed to feel this way. I just feel like I have the condemnation of God upon my life." But those feelings are not supposed to lead my life. What I **know** should lead the way. And I know that the Bible says that salvation is by grace through faith. I have trusted in Christ as my Savior. I am saved, therefore, by the truth of God's Word and not by how I feel. It is wonderful to "feel" saved, but my salvation is not based on whether I feel it or not. It is based on the Word of God — what I know!

When my daughter was very young, she had need for frequent correction. After being punished one day, she burst into tears. The correction was over; the punishment finished. And so I did not understand why she would be crying. I asked her. Her answer: "It doesn't feel like you love me." It is easy to see why she *felt* that way. Her disobedience had caused a situation that needed to be corrected. Correction never *feels* good. Because the correction came from me, it made her feel like I did not love her. She had the knowledge, however, that I did love her. She knew my love. The problem came when she allowed her feelings to lead. How often do we go through the same experience? Have you ever felt like God did not love you? Perhaps correction brought it about. Maybe difficult times tried to push those feelings to the front. Whatever the case, you need to be led by what you **know**. According to the Word of God, He does love you.

Casting all your care upon him; for he careth for you.
I Peter 5:7

For I am persuaded, that neither death, nor life, nor angels, nor principalities, nor powers, nor things present, nor things to come, Nor height, nor depth, nor any other creature, shall be able to separate us from the love of God, which is in Christ Jesus our Lord. Romans 8:38-39

How do you determine what is right or wrong? Thoughts and feelings should not be the deciding force. Take music for example. Worldly music can make you feel good. It can even make you feel happier when you are down. The beat and the sensation of it can pump you up and give you a feeling of confidence. But the fact that it can make you feel good does not make it right. The Word of God determines right from wrong. That is the knowledge by which you should be led.

Dearly beloved, I beseech you as strangers and pilgrims, abstain from fleshly lusts, which war against the soul.
I Peter 2:11

Love not the world, neither the things that are in the world. If any man love the world, the love of the Father is not in him.
I John 2:15

Pride is another example. It can feel good to be proud. If you let your feelings lead, you will embrace pride. It feels much better to think highly of yourself than to not think of yourself at all. It feels good to always be right. It feels good to think of yourself as better than other people. It can be enjoyable to tear others down verbally or mentally. I can remember a time I came home from visiting a friend. I felt so good. I had been such a help to her by pointing out her problems and telling her how to fix them. My high came crashing down, however, when I realized my feelings deceived me. I had not been a help to my friend. I had been proud. Pride is sin.

> *An high look, and a proud heart, and the plowing of the wicked, is sin.* Proverbs 21:4

How can something that feels so good be bad? Bad things can feel good because feelings can deceive. Feelings are not truth. Feelings are supposed to follow, not lead. Your assurance of salvation, the love of God, knowing right from wrong, or anything else needs to be led by what you know not what you feel. And that knowledge needs to come primarily from the Word of God.

Be led by faith not feelings.

Faith is not a feeling. It often produces feelings, but it is not a feeling. Unfortunately, when most people talk about faith, they really are focused on how they feel or want you to feel. "I just feel that God is going to get me out of this speeding ticket." "After singing five verses of Kum-ba-ya, I just have a peace in my heart that God will give me that million dollars I need." "You need more faith. Why, if you had enough faith you would mail that $25 check to us right now." Faith is promoted as something we must muster up within ourselves. But that is not Bible faith. Faith is taking

God at His Word. Because God said it, I believe it. Having faith about any particular thing is a decision.

Through faith we understand that the worlds were framed by the word of God, so that things which are seen were not made of things which do appear. Hebrews 11:3

Why do you believe that God created the heavens and the earth? It is through faith that you believe it. The Bible says it, and you made a decision to believe it. For most people, it was not a highly emotional experience. You likely did not shed any tears about your decision to believe in creation. There are some, however, that may have. I have heard of scientists who, after many years of promoting the theory of evolution, realized they were wrong. They changed their view and made a decision to believe in the creation of God. For them, it may have been a very emotional time. Is their belief in creation any greater than yours because they *felt* it? No. Faith is not a feeling.

I have wondered how Abraham felt when God told him to sacrifice his son Isaac. Surely he did not like the thought of it. He did not understand. He felt sad. I bet he had a big pit in his stomach and a lump in his throat. But he made a decision of faith. He chose to believe that God is in control, that His way is best, and that He would provide. As Abraham lifted the knife to kill his son, God gave him another way. Isaac was spared. If Abraham had been led by his feelings, do you think he would have been willing to sacrifice his son? No. He made sure his thoughts were following, not leading. Faith was his leader.

Janice was struggling with doubts about God and her salvation. These doubts flooded in when circumstances turned difficult. *"I want to believe God is there, but why is He letting this happen? It feels like He has forsaken me."* It is easy to stand back and be critical of this woman's lack of faith, but I know I have been there myself. Have you? To my shame, I have had those same thoughts before. Where is the victory in that? It is not in trying to overcome feelings. Victory comes with a decision to have faith—not to feel faith—but a decision that says, "I am going to take God at His Word. I am deciding to have faith that He *is* with me whether I feel like He is or not." In very difficult times, that decision of faith may need to be made daily, hourly, or sometimes by the minute. Victory only comes when you are led by faith—not feelings. Eventually, the feelings will follow. You will be able to say, "I feel like God is in control and is with me." It is nice to have that feeling there, but the feeling is secondary. Let faith lead.

Be led by obedience not feelings.

There are a lot of things in life that I do not feel like doing. Can you imagine a day when we did only that which felt good? Many of us would get out of bed only to get the ice cream out of the freezer. We do things all the time because they are right to do—not because we feel like doing them. Yet in many areas of our lives, we allow our feelings to lead. Take submission, for example. Does it always feel good to obey your parents? Obviously not! If you allow your emotions to be the leading force in your life, you will rebel. You need to make a decision to be led by obedience. Push those feelings back to the end of the line. You cannot fight the feelings and get rid of them on your own. But you can force them to mimic the leader. If the leader obeys, then the feelings will eventually change their view and follow.

This is a key truth in your relationship with young men. If you allow your emotions to lead your life, you are headed in a dangerous direction. Your feelings will want to have a close relationship with some particular guy. Your thoughts will try to convince you that you need that relationship. It feels so good to have him care for you. Those emotions will consume you and control all your decisions. You may get involved physically, though you would never intend for it to happen. You may marry a man that is not saved or serving God. Perhaps your marriage will end with a heartbreaking divorce. These tragic things do happen to Christian young women. Why do they make such unwise decisions? They do so because they have chosen to be led by feelings instead of obedience. A mess will always be the result of putting emotions in the lead. Push your feelings to the back of the line. Force them to follow. Though they may still be there, they do not need to have the leadership position.

I will never forget the day my husband came home early from work and broke the news to me. We were moving to Arizona. I was shocked. I felt overwhelmed and sad. I felt a great sense of loss. I loved our life the way it had been. I loved where we lived. I did not feel good about moving across the country to a place I did not know. There was nothing positive in my thoughts about it. There was nothing that *felt* good about it. But I also *knew* that it was God's will. I had to decide who would be the leader in my life: obedience or emotions. I could have put up such a fuss that my husband would decide not to go. But I knew that would be wrong. I submitted to it. And I cried.

Some would say, "If you were truly obedient about it, you would not have cried." I disagree. You see, feelings were not the leaders — they followed. The tears were okay. I was sad. It was hard. There was nothing wrong with feeling sad about it. *Sad* becomes wrong when *sad* leads. If I had kicked and screamed my way through the hard time, I would have been wrong. But I submitted, and then I cried. The tears did dry, and I soon came to think only good about the whole thing. I quickly came to love our new life in Arizona. The feelings followed my obedience. And even if they never came to agree with what God was clearly telling us to do, I would still have had the choice to follow obedience or emotions. You have that same choice in your life every day. Which is going to run your life? Who is going to be the leader?

Our lives as women do not need to be characterized by an unstable chasing of emotional butterflies. There will always be feelings. There will be days when tears come for no apparent reason. There are cycles and hormones that affect us. There are difficult circumstances that will come our way. Though the butterflies will flutter around, we do not need to chase them. We do not need to have them run our lives. Do not hate the butterflies. Just make sure you keep them where they belong — at the end of the line following along behind.

JOURNAL THOUGHTS

❑   I realize that I have been fighting against being the sensitive, emotional creature God has made. And I realize that emotional stability does not come from trying to eliminate my emotions altogether.

❑   I have been led by my feelings but now need to commit my works unto the Lord in these areas:

❑   I need to be led by what I know from God's Word instead of being led by my feelings concerning...

❑ I need to be led by faith instead of being led by my feelings concerning...

❑ I need to be led by obedience instead of being led by my feelings concerning...

CHAPTER FOURTEEN

Be the One Who Counts

As the twelve third graders rushed through the double glass doors, Kevin yelled out, "Let's play hide-and-seek!" Then with a running head start toward the playground, he added, "Last one to the slide is it."

In all my years of hide-and-seek playing, I do not recall an instance when someone volunteered to be the counter — to be "IT." There had to be some kind of race before the game could begin. Often it was simply a verbal "not it" race. And each time, the last one became the unlucky "IT." After all, who wants to be the counter? It is the boring and hard part of the game. How fun is it to close your eyes and count to one hundred? But even worse than that is the looking. No one wants to be "it" because it is not the best, fun part of the game. So kids sprint, push, and shove their way to the front to ensure they get what they want.

Unfortunately, we tend to live our lives the same way —

sprinting, pushing, and shoving to get what we want while trying to avoid the rest. We live selfishly. We make decisions to please ourselves. We say things to please ourselves. We do things to please ourselves. Our thoughts are about ourselves. Our dreams of the future revolve around ourselves. The focus of life is self. It sounds harsh, doesn't it? But recognition of the problem of selfishness is necessary if there is to be any hope for change.

When I was fifteen, I spent a summer working in a ministry that was staffed mostly by teenagers. Toward the end of the summer, there was an appreciation banquet in which each one of us received an award certificate for various attributes we portrayed throughout those few weeks. The award I received was for being self*less*. It made me feel good about myself. And for a long time I proudly thought that selfishness was not a problem I had. But time and the Word of God has convinced me otherwise. I have since thought how ironic that award was because selfishness is unquestionably one of the worst and most frequent problems of my life. While I am glad that my selfishness was not apparent to the leaders of that summer ministry, it does not negate the fact that much too much of my life has revolved around me.

Selfishness Has a Lot of Company

And the serpent said unto the woman, Ye shall not surely die: For God doth know that in the day ye eat thereof, then your eyes shall be opened, and ye shall be as gods, knowing good and evil. And when the woman saw that the tree was good for food, and that it was pleasant to the eyes, and a tree to be desired to make one wise, she took of the fruit thereof, and did eat, and gave also unto her husband with her; and he did eat. Genesis 3:4-6

Why did Eve disobey God by eating the fruit? Who was she thinking about? She was not thinking about God. She wasn't thinking about Adam. She wasn't thinking about future generations. She was thinking about herself.

When Cain, in Genesis chapter four, disobeyed God in his sacrifice and then in jealousy and rage killed his brother, who was he thinking about? Was it God? Was it his brother Abel? Was it his parents? Cain was living for himself!

The children of Israel murmured all through the wilderness. "No water. No food. Being a slave in Egypt was better than this. We want to go back." In their complaints it is obvious to see that they were focused on themselves.

The entire book of Jonah tells the story of a very selfish man. God told Jonah to go to Nineveh. But Jonah did not want to go and went to great lengths to avoid going. Later when God had mercy on the city of Nineveh, Jonah became angry at God because of it.

Therefore now, O LORD, take, I beseech thee, my life from me; for it is better for me to die than to live. Jonah 4:3

Then Jonah went outside the city, and sat down to see what would happen next. God caused a plant to grow over Jonah's head giving him shade from the hot sun. That plant made Jonah happy until God destroyed it. Then Jonah became angry again, saying, "It is better for me to die than to live."

And God said to Jonah, Doest thou well to be angry for the gourd? And he said, I do well to be angry, even unto death. Then said the LORD, Thou hast had pity on the gourd, for the which thou hast not laboured, neither madest it grow; which came up in a night, and perished in a night: And should not I spare Nineveh, that great city, wherein are more than sixscore thousand persons that cannot discern between their right hand and their left hand; and also much cattle? Jonah 4:9-11

Jonah was sprinting, pushing, and shoving to get what he wanted, not showing any sign of compassion toward the people of Nineveh or any care for God's will.

The problem of selfishness is not a new one; in fact, it has been passed down from generation to generation to the present day. We are born selfish. Have you been around babies or toddlers? No one had to teach them to think about themselves; they do it very naturally. They cry because they need or want something. They grab a desirable toy away from another child, triumphantly crying out, "Mine!" They throw tantrums when they do not get their way. As they grow up, their selfishness matures to become more socially accepted. In fact, our society today conditions us to ask the question, "What's in it for me?" about everything. Even as Christians, our flesh is consumed with satisfying self.

Of all his fellow servants at the time he wrote Philippians,

Paul found only one man whom he could trust to send to the Philippian people. The reason others were not qualified — selfishness.

> *But I trust in the Lord Jesus to send Timotheus shortly unto you, that I also may be of good comfort, when I know your state. For I have no man likeminded, who will naturally care for your state. For all seek their own, not the things which are Jesus Christ's.* Philippians 2:19-21

I like to think of myself as Timothy or Paul, not as one of these many self-seekers. But if you and I had been Paul's companions on that day, how would he have labeled us? Are we perhaps more self-centered than we realize? Here are some areas to examine.

Thoughts

Do you mutter in the silence of your mind what you would never dare say aloud? Do you fret over what other people are thinking about you? Do you pine after things that you do not have? Does it bring you great pleasure to see that a friend gained ten pounds over the summer? Is your way always the best and right way? Do you create mental scenarios of friends and family being unkind to you and then imagine how you would respond? Do you worry that something will come in the way of your happiness? Do you feel sorry for yourself? Do you find yourself noticing the faults of others? Do you assume you know what the other person is thinking, how they feel, and why they are doing what they are doing? Do you enjoy hearing and mulling over the juicy news you hear? Do you try to figure out ways to get people to notice you? Try to remember the thoughts you have had in the last day or two. What was the central theme? Who was in the middle of the majority of your thoughts?

Actions

Why do you do the things that you do? There are two pieces of pizza left. Selfishness takes the largest. Old friends of Mom and Dad pop in for a visit. Selfishness cannot wait for them to go home. There are three people using one bathroom. Selfishness has no regard for the other two people waiting for their turn. Mom is running behind and has supper to make, laundry to fold, and lunches to pack. Selfishness does not offer to help. Someone looks lonely sitting by herself. Selfishness ignores her. It is eleven at night at a hotel. Selfishness is loud and boisterous even though other guests may be trying to sleep. A sister is using the computer. Selfishness snaps at her that her time is up. There is a long weekend coming up, and it is announced that you are going to Grandma's house. Selfishness pouts because it interferes with more desirable plans. There is a handsome young man in the youth group. Selfishness cannot help but flirt a little. The alarm has gone off; Mom has reminded that it is time to get up. Selfishness sleeps a little longer. Little sister begs for some attention. Selfishness puts it off. A friend is over for the evening. Selfishness talks and talks but never listens.

Time

Much of your time is taken up with required activities like school and/or a job. Are you doing your best at it, or are you lazy? Laziness is a form of selfishness. The work may not be enjoyable, but if you are slothful in it, you are thinking of no one but self. What about your free time? Is it all spent watching TV, playing computer games, reading, shopping, sleeping in, talking on the phone, or just hanging out? Does an interruption to your schedule and your plans cause impatience, foul moods, and sometimes even panic? Do you waste much time due to lack of self-discipline in planning and organization? Do you procrastinate? Do you consider your time to be yours?

Relationships

Whom do you think about in your relationships? Who is the focus? How about with your parents? Is your goal to strive to honor, please, and love them? Or are you striving to get what you want from them while avoiding the rest? How about your relationship with your brothers and sisters? Are you seeking their best interest or your own? Who are you thinking about when you are with your friends—you or them? Why are you a friend to them? Is it because of the fun and companionship they can provide you? Why do you gravitate toward certain people while avoiding others? Is it because you are seeking the situations that are most socially comfortable to you, that bring you the most benefit and enjoyment? Whom are you thinking about when you come into contact with people that you do not even know? When you are at a store are you focusing on others in the checkout line or do you race to be first and then roll your eyes when the cashier is slow? How about when you are driving? Are you queen of the road? When you fail to give out a gospel tract or witness to an unsaved neighbor, who are you thinking about—you or them? What about your relationship with God? Is it all about Him and His will, or is it all about you and what you want?

Future

Examine your dreams and goals for the future. Likely, they are consumed with your interest and your happiness. You expect to secure a good paying job and look forward to the enjoyment a consistent income will bring *you*. You have pictured the ideal place to live based completely on what appeals to *you*. There is nothing wrong with the desire to get married. But even that good desire is likely all about *you* and *your* opinion about what will give *you* satisfaction. You desire to have children someday because of the joy it will bring *you*.

Taking time to give it some thought will reveal the unsettling truth that perhaps we are not the dedicated followers of Christ that we envisioned ourselves to be. Instead we too fit Paul's description.

> *For all seek their own, not the things which are Jesus Christ's.*
> Philippians 2:21

Selfishness Will Affect
Your Future Relationship...

With God

Demas had been a fellow servant alongside the apostles. He had undoubtedly been used by God. But selfishness prevailed in his life as Paul records.

For Demas hath forsaken me, having loved this present world.
II Timothy 4:10a

Demas loved the world because he loved himself. He sprinted toward what he wanted, leaving behind serving God because it conflicted with *his own* interests. As it caused Demas to forsake the service he was called to do, it will hinder you from fulfilling all God desires you to accomplish for Him. As it kept many of Paul's companions from being trusted to do an important task, so it will keep you from being qualified to do much of God's chosen work. Selfishness gets in the way of God's will. And in doing so it also gets in the way of true fulfillment and satisfaction.

With your parents

Selfishness will keep you from the good and honoring relationship that you should have with your parents — even when they are old and you are an adult. It is amazing how many Christian adults give no regard to their aging parents. They are not willing to slow down their own lives or put a dent in their personal savings in order to help their needy parents. Selfishness thinks that parents are the ones who are supposed to give time and money to their children. And if their parents can no longer do so, then there is no longer place for them in their lives. Do not convince yourself that you would never do such a thing if selfishness prevails in your relationship with your parents now.

With your friends

Selfishness will steal away your opportunity to be a good friend. Instead of being helpful during a trying time, you will be oblivious to your friend's need. You will want to talk about what is going on in your life without taking interest in hers. You will feel a need to compete with her — making sure your home is cleaner, your children are better educated, and your diet is successful — instead of encouraging her. You will be critical instead of supporting. You will be jealous instead of thankful for her blessings.

With your church

As a church member, selfishness will blind your eyes to the needs of others. You will either be no help in the programs of the church at all or complain because you feel like you do everything. Selfishness cannot look past the grimy clothes of the bus kids to see souls that need Christ. It will focus on the faults of the pastor and his family. Selfishness will only think about what the church can do for you instead of what you can do for the church.

With your children

A mother's job is to love, care for, and nourish her children. She will give of her time to feed, clothe, bathe, clean up after, and teach them. Those things alone require a level of selflessness. Yet a mother who does give much can still be guilty of selfishness in her relationship with her children. Selfishness does not stop to give discipline when it is needed. Selfishness has an unnecessarily sharp tongue of impatience. Selfishness forgets that a child has feelings that can be hurt. Selfishness never has time for reading a book or playing a game. It rejects the desire the child has to help in the kitchen because it will slow down dinner preparation and cause an extra mess. Selfishness does not have the patience to listen about a bad dream. Selfishness does not want to be bothered.

With your husband

The husband of a selfish wife can never meet her expectations. She easily notices and points out his faults. She fusses and complains about the things she feels are lacking in her life. Selfishness assumes. It grieves over not feeling loved instead of loving. Selfishness flippantly spends the money he has worked hard to provide and then complains when there is not enough. A selfish wife will boil up inside when her husband wants to attend a game or go golfing with his buddies. She will fail to meet his needs while working hard to make sure that he meets hers. She does not listen and later complains that he never talks to her. Selfishness is easily hurt. It is easily irritated. It is often defensive. Selfishness seeks its own happiness. And in the continual effort to satisfy, self can never seem to find that happiness for which it strives.

Ughhhhh!

You may feel hopeless. I admit there have been many times I have felt the same way. I am a selfish creature, and that selfishness destroys so much. I do not want to be that way. Is there any hope? Thankfully, all sin including selfishness and pride (the two really work side by side) will one day be forever left behind. As long as we remain in this flesh, we will battle with selfishness. There can exist, however, great victory. Let's look at some successful Bible examples.

There was an evil plot made against all the Jews of the land. In only a few days they were all to be destroyed. When Mordecai informed Esther his niece (but also queen) of the plot, she was grieved. Her people were to be destroyed. Mordecai asked her to go before the king and appeal to him for help. Esther was tempted to be selfish because she knew that to go before the king uninvited was potentially punishable by death. It was a dangerous thing to do. When Mordecai reminded her that both her life and the lives of all her family were at stake, Esther replied:

> *So will I go in unto the king, which is not according to the law: and if I perish, I perish.* Esther 4:16b

She made the decision to give up her life in an effort to save her people. She set aside selfishness, and she and her people were spared.

Naomi and her two daughters-in-law had all lost their husbands. Naomi decided to go back to her homeland and people. She told her daughters-in-law to stay in Moab with their own families. It would be the easiest and most natural thing to do. One daughter-in-law did go back to her pagan family, but Ruth said:

> *Intreat me not to leave thee, or to return from following after thee: for whither thou goest, I will go; and where thou lodgest, I will lodge: thy people shall be my people, and thy God my God: Where thou diest, will I die, and there will I be buried: the LORD do so to me, and more also, if ought but death part thee and me.* Ruth 1:16-17

Not only did Ruth selflessly stick by her mother-in-law's side and follow her to a land that was foreign to her, but she also went right to work to support, yes herself, but also her mother-in-law. To add to it, Naomi had become bitter because of the death of her husband and two sons. She would not have been a fun person to live with. Ruth was not living for herself.

Who can find a virtuous woman? for her price is far above rubies. The heart of her husband doth safely trust in her, so that he shall have no need of spoil. She will do him good and not evil all the days of her life. She seeketh wool, and flax, and worketh willingly with her hands. She is like the merchants' ships; she bringeth her food from afar. She riseth also while it is yet night, and giveth meat to her household, and a portion to her maidens. She considereth a field, and buyeth it: with the fruit of her hands she planteth a vineyard. She girdeth her loins with strength, and strengtheneth her arms. She perceiveth that her merchandise is good: her candle goeth not out by night. She layeth her hands to the spindle, and her hands hold the distaff. She stretcheth out her hand to the poor; yea, she reacheth forth her hands to the needy. She is not afraid of the snow for her household: for all her household are clothed with scarlet. She maketh herself coverings of tapestry; her clothing is silk and purple. Her husband is known in the gates, when he sitteth among the elders of the land. She maketh fine linen, and selleth it; and delivereth girdles unto the merchant. Strength and honour are her clothing; and she shall rejoice in time to come. She openeth her mouth with wisdom; and in her tongue is the law of kindness. She looketh well to the ways of her household, and eateth not the bread of idleness. Her

children arise up, and call her blessed; her husband also, and
he praiseth her. Many daughters have done virtuously, but
thou excellest them all. Proverbs 31:10-29

Why is the virtuous woman so remarkable? Why do we, as we read of her, greatly respect her? We have never met her, yet we are awed by her life. While much could be said about her, one thing is crystal clear—she was selfless. She did her husband good, and not evil *all the days of her life.* In her marriage, she was living for him. It was not about what he could do for her; it was all about what she could do for him. She was not concerning herself with her own needs, but his. She did not fuss at him. She did not speak unkindly. She lived for him. She was not selfish with her time, but worked hard in many different areas. She got up early in the morning when it would have been more pleasant to sleep a little longer. Why did she get up? To feed her family and servants! If I had servants, I think I would sleep a little longer while they made breakfast for me. But she arose early to make sure everybody in her house was provided for. She helped the poor and needy. She was compassionate toward others. In her tongue was the law of kindness—never an unkind word muttered! She feared the Lord, putting His will before her own. It is no wonder that her husband and children called her blessed. A remarkable woman she certainly was. Why? Because she did not live her life for herself! Her thoughts, actions, time, and relationships were all about others. She was not a self-seeker. She had made the decision to be *the one who counts.* And in doing so, she *did count*! She was chosen by God to be an example to us all.

John the Baptist was famous. He had a large following. But when the people began turning from him to follow Jesus, some of John's disciples complained about it. What was John the Baptist's reply?

He must increase, but I must decrease. John 3:30

A selfish person would at least feel jealous about someone else stealing all the attention. But John understood that the Son of God was far greater than he. He knew the whole point of his job was to point to Jesus. It was not all about John; it was all about Christ.

Paul was misunderstood, accused, beaten, shipwrecked, imprisoned, and put to death. Why did he put up with it all? He answered that question in Philippians.

For to me to live is Christ, and to die is gain. Philippians 1:21

His whole life was not about himself; it was about Christ. His thoughts, his actions, his time, his relationships, his future—all of it was about Christ. Everything! *For to me to live is Christ.* We so easily quote the verse, often personalizing it, yet how little its meaning sinks in. Can I honestly say that? Everything—about Christ. None about me? How amazing Paul was!

Through Christ

These men and women all saw victory over selfishness. They give us an example so that we may know it is possible. But it was not Esther or Ruth who accomplished it. Neither was it John or Paul. And it will not be through you or me either. Hopefully, we have been stirred up to see that we are selfish and need to change. Our human tendency, however, will keep us from the victory we want. You see, what I am likely to do with my conviction is to sit up straight and tall and proclaim, "That's it! I am not going to be selfish anymore. From now on I am going to be like the Proverbs 31 woman!" And then I will try to accomplish it. And do you know what will happen? I will fall flat on my face! I will fail and continue on living in my selfishness feeling hopeless about it all.

Victory is never achieved by pulling *myself* up by the boot straps. Through *self*-confidence. Through *self*-help. Through *self*-dependence. Through *my* sheer determination. Through any thing that *I* can do. Victory will only come when I allow someone else to do in me what I could never do on my own.

> *Let this mind be in you, which was also in Christ Jesus: Who, being in the form of God, thought it not robbery to be equal with God: But made himself of no reputation, and took upon him the form of a servant, and was made in the likeness of men: And being found in fashion as a man, he humbled himself, and became obedient unto death, even the death of the cross.*
> Philippians 2:5-8

The Creator allowed Himself to be beaten, scorned, and cruelly put to death by His own creatures. Why? So that they could have hope. So that they could have His righteousness. None of it was for Himself. It was all for you. Almighty God gave His everything. He was perfect in His self*less*ness. He was the one perfect example. Never selfish! He had success and victory every time. And He is completely qualified and capable of accomplishing the same in you.

You can have victory over selfishness. (And by the way, over any other sin problem as well.) How? The answer is Philippians 4:13.

> *I can do all things through Christ which strengtheneth me.*
> Philippians 4:13

This is a popular verse among Christians, but often believers emphasize the wrong part. In fact, they miss the whole point. The emphasis is not: **I** *can do all things.* It is: **through Christ**. Jesus Himself tells us the following:

> *I am the vine, ye are the branches: He that abideth in me, and I in him, the same bringeth forth much fruit: <u>for without me ye can do nothing.</u>* John 15:5

Do you want victory over selfishness? Ask God to do in you what you could never accomplish on your own. Commit the matter to him daily, hourly, and by the minute. *For to me to live is Christ* is not a statement of Paul's determination. It is a statement of truth about Paul's life. His life was Christ's life. His mind was the mind of Christ. How? He yielded himself, abiding in complete dependence upon the One Who is perfect victory.

How I long to be rid of this selfishness that plagues me! Do you want the same? May God enable us to be *ones who count!*

JOURNAL THOUGHTS

I realize that I have been selfish...
❑   In my thoughts. (Be specific.)

❑   In my actions. (Be specific.)

❑   In my time. (Be specific.)

❑   In my relationships. (Be specific.)

❑   In my plans for the future. (Be specific.)

❑   I am making the decision to confess these sins of selfishness to God.

❑   I want my selfishness to turn to selflessness, but I acknowledge that it can never be accomplished by my own efforts. I am making the decision to depend on Christ to fulfill this in me. (Ask Him for it daily.)

CHAPTER FIFTEEN
If Only

In 1849 hundreds of people packed up what they could and deserted their homes, jobs, belongings, and even families to head west. They had heard the widespread rumor that there was gold out there—and lots of it too. They left all behind and spent weeks, months, and years searching for what? Gold, wealth, a better life? All that is true. But what they were truly seeking was happiness.

In 1513, Ponce De Leon discovered what is now the state of Florida. But Florida was not what he was looking for. He had heard stories of a fountain of youth; he set his heart on finding it. What would it mean for him? Certainly riches. Perhaps good health and long life. Maybe it would even stop the aging process altogether. But his true search was for something more—it was for happiness.

In 2006, Beth left her apartment complex for the last time. She was fourteen and tired of her life the way it was. Her family was a wreck. Her school a bore. Where was she going? Of the exact location she was not sure, but it was a place where she could find the love and excitement for which she longed.

We know the end of all the stories, don't we! Some did strike it rich in California, and some did not. But none struck happiness. Ponce De Leon's explorations were very beneficial, but he never found what he was looking for — neither the Fountain of Youth nor happiness. Beth's circumstances did drastically change. While she did run away from home, she could never seem to run away from her unhappiness. How foolish of these people to think that searching for gold, for youth, or for love and excitement would bring them happiness. We know better! Or do we?

Are you satisfied? I do not mean, "Are you having a good day?" I do not mean, "Do you have it pretty good?" I do not mean, "Do you at this moment have a pleasant feeling?" I mean, "Are you satisfied with your life the way it is?" Or is there something lacking in your general, overall happiness? Many people, if they were completely honest, would say that, yes, there is something missing. And many could continue on to name the thing that is lacking. What about you? What are you lacking? What is it that would make you happy? To change your looks? Getting married? More popularity? Better grades? A stable home situation? Improved health? A car? More friends? A little more spending money? To go to college? More ability? What is it that you long for? What is it that would bring you happiness right now if only you had it? It could be as simple as a Little Debbie® Swiss Cake Roll (my personal favorite). While it does taste good and may even cure my craving for something sweet, it has never brought me happiness—a short-lived moment of bliss, perhaps, but not that overall feeling of satisfaction that I desire. It will not for you either. Deep inside we all know these things cannot bring us true happiness, yet so often we seek them, long for them. We live "if only" lives.

If Only I *WERE*...

If only I were prettier!

As an average looking person, I know how you feel. I have spent a lot of time in my years wishing I had a little more beauty. When I have observed the glowing skin, bouncing-beautiful hair, and thin figures of those around me, I have often caught myself thinking, *"If only I were prettier – more like..."* and then I name someone I know or have seen. It is true that appearance is important. We should improve when we can. We should make sure we do not look sloppy. Lose some weight, change a hair style—all of that is fine and good. But to mope our lives away because we are only average looking instead of one of the beautiful ones is nothing short of pride and selfishness.

Yes—pride! Usually we think of pride as something that happens to people who have great talent, beauty, or wealth. Many famous sports players are cocky and proud. Many glamorous Hollywood stars are conceited. People with lots of money often are guilty of turning up their noses at other people. While all of this is true, pride can also be more subtle. It can come in the form of self-pity as well. Why is it that you want to be better looking than you are? For whose benefit would it be? It is about you and only about you. You are not satisfied with the way God made you. You want the attention, glory, and favor that you think beauty will bring you. You feel as if you deserve better than what you have. You want to be at the top with your looks. It does sound selfish and proud, doesn't it?

Let nothing be done through strife or vainglory; but in lowliness of mind let each esteem other better than themselves. Look not every man on his own things, but every man also on the things of others. Let this mind be in you, which was also in Christ Jesus: Who, being in the form of God, thought it not robbery to be equal with God: But made himself of no reputation, and took upon him the form of a servant, and was made in the likeness of men:...Do all things without murmurings and disputings. Philippians 2:3-7, 14

Notice the word *vainglory* in verse three. Then consider what Proverbs 31 has to say about beauty.

Favour is deceitful, and beauty is vain: but a woman that feareth the LORD, she shall be praised. Proverbs 31:30

You desire beauty—something God says is vain. And furthermore you desire it so you can have the favor of man—something God says is deceitful. Your longings to be prettier are really longings for vainglory—or empty pride.

Empty pride will never bring you satisfaction. If I had the

magical ability to change how you and I look and make us into gorgeous women, we would not be made happy by it. Oh, I imagine our flesh would enjoy the human attention it would bring. We might feel short bursts of glee. But we would not be satisfied by our beauty. No, beauty can never bring contentment. After all, it is vain.

If only I were more talented, more personable, or smarter! Is there anything wrong with working to broaden our talents? Or to increase our knowledge? Or to improve our social skills? Of course not! But that is not the issue here. We are addressing the "if only" attitude that wishes to be what we are not. Why do you or I pine after that talent and ability that we see in someone else? Why do we long to have the personality of another? Is it because we want to be able to serve God more fully? To be used by Him? No, really it is the same the reason that we desire beauty. We want to be known. We want attention. We want vainglory.

"But," we say, "if only God had endued me with that talent, then I could do so much more for Him." We need to ask ourselves, "Is that really what God wants us to do?" I have a friend who is musically challenged. He cannot carry a tune in a bucket. There is no working to make it better; he is tone deaf. Do you think God created him to be a song leader in a church? "Of course not!" we would say. "If God wanted that He would have given him at least some natural music ability or miraculously changed his lack of it." God called my friend to do something different. And my friend is good at what he does, *very* good. He developed the gift God created in him and can now serve in exactly the way

God wanted. By the way, my friend's service is not a "lime-light" type of work. It is a "behind the scenes" job. "But," we want to argue, "if he could sing he could have...." Could have done what? Be up in front of a lot of people? Impress a crowd? I am thankful he is willing to do exactly what God wants him to do—human recognition or not.

> *It is not good to eat much honey: so for men to search their own glory is not glory.* Proverbs 25:27

If Only I *HAD*...

If only I had possessions!
What is it? A car of your own, a computer, nicer or more clothes? How about your own phone, a piano, enough money to buy a school lunch instead of bringing peanut butter and jelly every day? Or maybe it is that new pair of shoes, an updated music player, or a horse. Perhaps it is a room of your own. What is the thing for which you pine? How much money or stuff do you want? Would getting it bring you happiness and satisfaction?

> *Better is little with the fear of the LORD than great treasure and trouble therewith.* Proverbs 15:16

> *Better is a little with righteousness than great revenues without right.* Proverbs 16:8

> *A good name is rather to be chosen than great riches, and loving favour rather than silver and gold.* Proverbs 22:1

The Word of God tells us that it is better to have the fear of the Lord, righteousness, and a good name than it is to have riches. In other words, these three things are of more value to you and your satisfaction in life than anything on your *if only I had* list. In fact, Proverbs also gives a description of your want list.

> *Labour not to be rich: cease from thine own wisdom. Wilt thou set thine eyes upon that which is not? for riches certainly make themselves wings; they fly away as an eagle toward heaven.*
> Proverbs 23:4-5

It does not last. A car, clothes, money, music, a room—it does not matter what it is. Proverbs here tells us not to set our eyes on temporal things. How could something God warns us about possibly bring us satisfaction?

Let me pause to say that I am not suggesting that it is wrong to have a computer, a horse, or a new outfit. My husband and I have been praying that God will provide us with a personal computer. We desire to have one because we feel it would be a real asset as we strive to serve God, and we desire to teach our children much needed computer skills. But we are not seeking a computer because we think it will make us happy. In fact, if God decides that it would be better that we not have one, it would be no big deal. We would not be crushed. We would not fret over it. There is a big difference between that attitude and *If only I had...then I would be happy.*

Lay not up for yourselves treasures upon earth, where moth and rust doth corrupt, and where thieves break through and steal: But lay up for yourselves treasures in heaven, where neither moth nor rust doth corrupt, and where thieves do not break through nor steal: For where your treasure is, there will your heart be also....No man can serve two masters: for either he will hate the one, and love the other; or else he will hold to the one, and despise the other. Ye cannot serve God and mammon. Therefore I say unto you, Take no thought for your life, what ye shall eat, or what ye shall drink; nor yet for your body, what ye shall put on. Is not the life more than meat, and the body than raiment?...(For after all these things do the Gentiles seek:) for your heavenly Father knoweth that ye have need of all these things. But seek ye first the kingdom of God, and his righteousness; and all these things shall be added unto you. Matthew 6:19-21, 24-25, 32-33*

There are Christians whose lives are characterized by a love of stuff. Money and the things it can buy are the primary focus of their lives. They seek treasure and their heart is with that treasure instead of with God. According to verse 24, it is not possible to serve the love of money and God at the same time. If a person is serving money, she is not serving God. The passage continues to warn us not to focus on or worry about material things, even such basic needs of life as food, water, and clothing. If we are not to be consumed with even these essentials, it would also make sense that we should not be consumed with the less necessary wants of our life. Verse 33 contrasts our fleshly tendency to focus on things by exhorting us to first seek God.

This issue will make an impact on your future. I know of ladies who were so consumed with a nice house and certain style of living that they refused to follow their husbands into the ministry that God was calling them to. In some cases, husbands have felt such a pressure to maintain their wife's financial expectations that they work overtime instead of making sure their family is going to and serving in a local church. Other couples began married life serving God but stopped—all for the love of money, all because they felt they could not be happy without a certain set of material things. If you have battled being consumed with "stuff" and do not deal with the problem now, you may find yourself following after riches all your life without ever experiencing the satisfaction of doing God's will.

> *If ye then be risen with Christ, seek those things which are above, where Christ sitteth on the right hand of God. Set your affection on things above, not on things on the earth. For ye are dead, and your life is hid with Christ in God.* Colossians 3:1-3

If only I had different circumstances!
Your family situation may be less than ideal. A different and better situation, however, cannot provide you with true satisfaction. School may come hard for you. Perhaps you work and work at it only to barely pass. Having it be easier would not give you happiness. It could be that you feel lonely and dream for a good friend. The fulfilling of your dream, however, is not capable of filling the void. You may have a legitimate and even serious health problem. There is no question but that it is a difficult circumstance. But

healing in and of itself will not give you true satisfaction. If your longing was filled this very minute, you would find yourself longing for something else within weeks.

Paul desired to be rid of his eye problems and prayed for healing. God said "no" because it was not His will to heal Paul. Did Paul wallow in self pity? Was his satisfaction dependent upon his health? No! Paul responded by saying,

> *Most gladly therefore will I rather glory in my infirmities, that the power of Christ may rest upon me.*
> II Corinthians 12:9b

Hannah longed for a child. She had a barren womb yet desired to be a mother. She asked God to give her a child. God said, "Yes." He gave her Samuel along with several other children. Did Hannah find true satisfaction? I suspect yes! But that satisfaction did not come from her children. Listen to the beginning of Hannah's prayer after she gave Samuel to be a servant of Eli, the high priest.

> *My heart rejoiceth in the LORD, mine horn is exalted in the LORD: my mouth is enlarged over mine enemies; because I rejoice in thy salvation. There is none holy as the LORD: for there is none beside thee: neither is there any rock like our God.* I Samuel 2:1b-2

Notice what she said in verse 2. *There is none beside thee.* Were the children a blessing? Unquestionably, yes! Were there many happy times with those children? For sure! Was Hannah truly satisfied by those children? No! Her satisfaction was in the One Who gave her the blessing.

Is it legitimate for you to pray for different circumstances? Sure it is! But remember, your satisfaction is not dependent upon a change in those circumstances.

If Only My Future Were... NOW!

In college it was not unusual to see some sort of handmade countdown calendar hung on the outside of several dorm rooms toward the end of April, when seniors were soon to be graduates. They were excited. They were almost done with school forever. And they were looking toward that day with anticipation.

On the first of December, we hang a Christmas tree countdown calendar. Each day, the kids love pulling out a felt ornament and hanging it on the little tree. It is an exciting time looking forward to Christmas Day.

The twenty-four-year-old young man is passed in the hall by one of his buddies who asks, "How much longer?" "Thirteen days, four hours, thirty-nine minutes, and......ten seconds," he replies. He knows exactly how long until his upcoming wedding. He is excited. He is looking forward to it.

We all have times when we are anticipating an exciting future event. It can add to the excitement to count down the days. It is fun to think and dream about the future. While there is nothing wrong with that anticipation, and while it certainly is important to prepare for the future, we do need to guard ourselves from the temptation to wish our lives away. Just as the grass seems greener on the other side of the fence, the future can look brighter, more exciting, and more rewarding than today does. Then when you arrive at that future, there is something else to look forward to; and you begin wishing toward that time. On and on you wish.

An eight-year-old wishes she were ten because it would be neat to be an age with two digits in it. A ten-year-old wishes to be twelve because there is something magical about twelve. A twelve-year-old pines after thirteen and the beginning of the teen years. A thirteen-year-old cannot wait for sixteen and the keys to the car. A sixteen-year-old looks toward eighteen when she will be considered a legal adult. An eighteen-year-old cannot wait until she is through with school. A college graduate greatly anticipates marriage. A young married couple looks forward to the addition of children. A mother with young children looks forward to the day she will no longer have to change diapers. And with each wish for the future is an assumption that the next stage of life will make her happy. Likely, somewhere during her thirties or forties she will realize that she has wished much of her life away and will begin to wish it back again.

Being a homeschool mother, I found myself counting down the days until summer break. After a couple years of doing this, it dawned on me that summer breaks really did not last long, and soon we were into the next school year. If I continued wishing school days by, I would be wishing my kids' lives away. And I am in no hurry to have them grow up and leave me. I have since stopped focusing on summer break and have decided to enjoy every day with my children—school days and all. Time goes by quickly enough. I want to take advantage of each day that I have with them.

If you are not careful, you will succumb to the temptation to wish your days away. Be glad for *this* day that the Lord has given you.

Rejoice evermore. 1 Thessalonians 5:16

Rejoice in the Lord alway: and again I say, Rejoice. Philippians 4:4

Yes, prepare for tomorrow. Go ahead and dream a little too. But do not look toward your future as an escape from the unhappiness you have today. Tomorrow cannot and will not bring you satisfaction.

Filling the Void

Paul had been beaten, imprisoned, bitten by a snake, shipwrecked, and was in constant danger of being killed. He had experienced times of great poverty. He was often separated from his closest friends. And yet he said:

Not that I speak in respect of want: for I have learned, in whatsoever state I am, therewith to be content. I know both how to be abased, and I know how to abound: every where and in all things I am instructed both to be full and to be hungry, both to abound and to suffer need. Philippians 4:11-12

How did he do it? How was it that he could be content even though much about his life was less than ideal? Where did he find true satisfaction? The answer is found in the next verse.

I can do all things through Christ which strengtheneth me. Philippians 4:13

Strength to bear anything that comes our way comes *through Christ.* True satisfaction comes *through Christ.*

For he satisfieth the longing soul, and filleth the hungry soul with goodness. Psalm 107:9

I am reminded of the beautiful song.

Only Jesus can satisfy your soul;
And only He can change your heart and make you whole.
He'll give you peace you never knew,
Sweet love and joy, and Heaven too;
For only Jesus can satisfy your soul![1]

Love, joy, and peace — isn't that what you and I truly want? Isn't that how we imagine being satisfied would be? It never comes come from fulfilling our *if onlys.* It comes as we yield to the Spirit of God and choose to abide in Christ. It is true that only He can satisfy and He is enough!

> *Let your conversation be without covetousness; and be content*
> *with such things as ye have: for he hath said, I will never leave*
> *thee, nor forsake thee. So that we may boldly say, The Lord is*
> *my helper, and I will not fear what man shall do unto me.*
> Hebrews 13:5-6

JOURNAL THOUGHTS

❑   I have been guilty of living an "if only I were prettier, more talented, more personable, or smarter" life and am making the decision to confess this sin of pride to God. With His help, I am finished feeling sorry for myself because of:

❑   I have been consumed with money and possessions and am making the decision to confess my covetousness to God. I realize that these things, for which I have pined, can never bring me satisfaction:

❑   I have been wasting my days wishing for these different circumstances:

❑   I have been so consumed in my anticipation for the future that I have been dissatisfied with this stage of my life. I am making the decision that with God's help, I will make the most of every day that He gives me.

❑   I realize that true satisfaction comes only through Christ. I am making the decision to seek after Him and the love, joy, and peace that can only come by abiding/depending on Him.